THE INSIGHT EDGE

THE INSIGHT EDGE

An Introduction to the Theory and Practice of Evolutionary Management

Ervin Laszlo and Christopher Laszlo

Foreword by James Ogilvy

QUORUM BOOKS
Westport, Connecticut • London

658
L34;

Library of Congress Cataloging-in-Publication Data

Laszlo, Ervin, 1932–
   The insight edge : an introduction to the theory and practice of
evolutionary management / Ervin Laszlo and Christopher Laszlo ;
foreword by James Ogilvy.
      p. cm.
   Includes bibliographical references and index.
   ISBN 1–56720–096–6 (alk. paper)
   1. Industrial management.   I. Laszlo, Christopher.   II. Title.
HD30.19.L37   1997
658—dc20   96–9049

British Library Cataloguing in Publication Data is available.

Library of Congress Catalog Card Number: 96–9049
ISBN: 1–56720–096–6

First published in 1997

Quorum Books, 88 Post Road West, Westport, CT 06881
An imprint of Greenwood Publishing Group, Inc.

Printed in the United States of America

∞™

The paper used in this book complies with the
Permanent Paper Standard issued by the National
Information Standards Organization (Z39.48–1984).

10 9 8 7 6 5 4 3 2 1

Contents

Figures

Foreword

As if it were not enough to have blazed its way into intellectual history by revolutionizing our perception of man's place in nature, evolutionary theory has now come to dominate our way of thinking about much more than the origin of species and the descent of man. We are now beginning to see how the concept of evolution covers not only the long history of species discovered by paleontologists, but also the growth and development of other complex systems, from language to the economy.

Like the Copernican revolution, which not only revised our thoughts about the heavens but also had repercussions here on earth, so ideas about the evolution of biological species kicked off a whole series of repercussions in other fields—repercussions that are still sounding and whose echoes are yet to be heard. Not only does evolutionary theory transfer us from a fundamentally static, ahistorical worldview inherited from Plato and Aristotle and hurl humanity very much into time, but it also changes our ideas about change itself. In place of the Hellenic teleological view of things becoming what they were supposed to become, and of the Newtonian mechanistic view of effects necessarily following from causes, evolutionary theory leads us to think in terms of a complex dynamic made up of random variation and environmental selection. By allowing us neither the sublime eternity of Christian Platonism nor the precise determinism of Newtonian mechanics, evolutionary theory throws us into time and leaves us permanently under the shadow of chance. Things don't happen because it's for the best. Nor do they follow as predictable and controllable effects of causes. Things happen because they end up being selected from a welter of alternatives by a welter of competing influences operating on many registers and rhythms at the same time. This untidy, yet ultimately functional, picture of the (dis)order of things begins to sound very much like the world of business and the marketplace.

Business executives have been rightly skeptical about many academic approaches to the pragmatic complexities of the marketplace. To the extent that academicians come with clipboards and elegant models and theories about the way things are supposed to work, the response is likely to be something like, "that may be the way it goes in theory, but in practice . . .". And if academics add bells and whistles to their theory to take care of the exceptions that occur in practice, then their theory, which may have been originally oversimple, may become too complex to be of use.

But contemporary evolutionary theory reverses the entire relationship between business and academia. The theory itself is incredibly simple, and the more you apply it, the more complexity it accommodates. Rather than predicting a particular state description on the basis of a covering law and a prior state description, evolutionary theory explains without rigid, single-outcome predicting. It grants the chaos and the mess and the randomness in things, then says that whatever evolves out of the mess did so—and will continue to do so—because it was able to coevolve with other parts of the mess. Evolutionary theory is a way of thinking, not so much about linear sequences of deterministic causes and effects, but about the systematic relationships that interrelate things with their environments. It is intrinsically holistic and relational rather than linear and mechanistic.

Evolutionary thinking always looks at things in context: a species adapting to an ecological niche, a new product responding to an unmet need. The perspective of evolutionary theory is always and inevitably temporal and dynamic on the one hand, and holistic and environmental on the other. By forcing this 360-degree view of the environment, evolutionary thinking widens any perspective that is locked into the linear tunnel vision of simple causes and effects. For this reason, evolutionary thinking is useful for policy makers and executives who know the need for 360-degree vision.

Once one becomes habituated to take an evolutionary perspective on things, it is quite amazing how revelatory and fruitful this perspective can be in the world of business and politics. We have now come far beyond the crudities of the early chapters of Herbert Spencer's social Darwinism and the survival of the fittest. Contemporary evolutionary theory has come to appreciate the survival value of cooperation among coevolving species in symbiotic relationship. Further, where evolutionary theory is applied to intelligent organisms that have recording systems such as culture, it is clear that acquired characteristics—customs—can be inherited. Evolutionary thinking applied to human systems then begins to look more like social Lamarckianism than the old bugaboo of social Darwinism.

The authors of this book are uniquely qualified to shed light on the interpretation and application of the latest developments in evolutionary theory. Ervin Laszlo has published widely on systems theory and is the founder of what is becoming widely known as general evolution theory. And he has immersed himself in the ways of the world with years of work as director of research at the United Nations as scientific guru of the Vienna Academy, and now as founder and president of the Club of Budapest. Christopher Laszlo is a successful young practioner, applying evolutionary thinking in his job as head of business development for Central Europe in the French-based Fortune 500 company Lafarge.

The book they have written comes at a crucial time. Its subject speaks to the needs of the time.

James Ogilvy
President, Global Business Network

Preface

This book has been written to bring a fresh and presently much-needed insight to managers based on knowledge developed in the new sciences of complexity and chaos. In times of turbulence, when the business environment is in rapid evolution hallmarked by increasingly global competition, new and rapidly changing products and technologies, mounting ecologic and social challenges and responsibilities, and broad changes in consumer values, the knowledge coming from these sciences provides executives with an informed perspective that can be developed into a reliable guide to action. In the last decade of the twentieth century, evolutionary systems dynamics has acquired unique relevance and potentially unmatched utility for effective business management.

Evolutionary knowledge does not emerge from the new sciences, like Venus from the sea, complete and functional in every detail. Genuine evolutionary insight requires a process of distillation from a base that is complex and seemingly esoteric; it might take considerable time to evolve from it relevant business applications. Even if they have the ability, managers cannot spare the time to perform this task. A collaborative effort is needed between scientists and businesspeople. Scientists need to select concepts and theories of potential business relevance from the state-of-the-art knowledge base, and business executives need to review the resulting information and adapt it to their needs so that it is operational and to the point.

Collaboration of this kind is yet to be achieved in regular practice. In this book, however, a beginning has been made. The present team of authors, one of whom comes from the sciences and the other from business, have collaborated for years. For a number of years, each was ac-

quainted with the field of expertise and activity of the other—they
happen to be father and son. In the last few years, the first author had
considerable contact with managers, who turned to him in increasing
numbers for advice and ideas. And the second author, having been entrusted with general management responsibilities in his company, has
had occasion to apply evolutionary principles in the practical context of
multinational corporate management. This book owes its existence to the
realization that in our turbulent times such collaboration can make a real
contribution to effective business practice. The authors hope that its publication may bring fresh insights to business executives and to all others
concerned with effective and responsible business practice.

Part I

New Thinking
for a New World

One cannot solve a problem with the same kind of thinking that gave rise to that problem.

—Albert Einstein

Chapter 1

Renewing the Managerial Knowledge Base

Current management lore abounds with exhortations for managers to become brainy and acquire the relevant kinds of business knowledge. The key capital, according to Ernst & Young's Center for Business Innovation, is intellectual material that has been formalized, captured, and leveraged to produce a higher-valued asset. Harvard management guru Shoshana Zuboff agrees. She writes in her *In the Age of the Smart Machine* that one of the principal purposes of the modern enterprise is the expansion of knowledge—not knowledge for its own sake, but knowledge that comes to reside at the core of what it means to be productive. The behaviors that define learning and the behaviors that define being productive are one and the same: learning is the heart of productive activity.[1]

In today's turbulent business environment, advice like this is well taken. It becomes clearer by the day that if managers are to get to the top, and if they are to stay on top, they must be open to effective business knowledge. The question is: What is this knowledge, and how can managers access it?

In this opening chapter we provide a thumbnail sketch of three different kinds of business knowledge. Readers can then judge their comparative utility for themselves.

THE THREE KINDS OF BUSINESS KNOWLEDGE

The first of the existing kinds of business knowledge is knowledge about the company and its industry: the relevant human, financial, and organizational resources, together with the needs of collaborators, customers, suppliers, and distributors. This is the classical knowledge base, and it is by no means extinct: it resides at the core of many a short- and medium-term effort at focused cost-cutting and value-adding. While such measures are often good and sometimes necessary, when carried out without due regard for such factors as organizational adaptability, personnel learning ability, and the strategic foresight that must give them direction, they may ultimately fail. Attempting to steer a 1990s enterprise by the company-centered methods of conventional management is like concentrating all one's skills on flying an airplane and paying scant attention to which airspace one is flying in. Today's captains cannot be solely concerned with the internal functioning of their aircraft: they must also set a course in reference to climatic conditions, current position and projected destination, and the traffic on the network of routes crisscrossing the globe. That traffic is diversified and complex. It includes customers, competitors, suppliers, distributors, R&D partners, technology subcontractors, governmental departments and ministries, and many other craft.

The second kind of business knowledge includes familiarity with the new "hard" and "soft" operative technologies. In the 1980s and early 1990s, this has meant placing emphasis on information technology and the processes by which information is diffused and communicated both *within* the enterprise and *between* the enterprise and its clients, customers, suppliers, and distributors. This kind of knowledge sheds light on the issues and forces that impact on markets and labor forces as well as on client and consumer preferences; it provides access not only to the functions and operations of the company, but also to some elements of its social and ecological environment. It is an improvement on the first, but it, too, is inadequate to cope with a rapidly changing business environment.

Business knowledge of the third kind includes, in addition to the above two kinds, a working insight into the *dynamics* that drives change in today's rapidly evolving and increasingly interdependent economic and social world. By and large, this knowledge is still lacking in contemporary business circles. The factors that drive change and transformation in the world, if known at all, are known mainly by intuition by a handful of managers endowed with extraordinary business sense. This can, of course, produce notable results: nobody can deny the importance of vision and intuition in the conduct of contemporary businesses. But ongoing competitiveness in major companies calls for a knowledge base that is more reliable than personal intuition on the part of the individual at or near the top. It calls for genuine and reliable insight, accessed and shared by the entire management team. Companies today have taken on the properties of complex dynamical systems, and such systems, while not responsive to being "driven" from above, are entirely capable of being insightfully orchestrated, and purposefully navigated over highly complex terrains.

In the past, business knowledge of the first kind sufficed for all intents and purposes—companies had not yet acquired the characteristics of complex self-evolving systems; they were not as yet fully embedded in national and transnational economic, social, and ecological processes. Since globalization, communication, and interdependence were less pronounced, even for making strategic decisions it was enough to factor in the local setting's parameters: its demand patterns, customer preferences, competitors, and suppliers. This has changed. In today's world, the key success factors focus on the interactions between the complex system that is the organization, and its likewise complex operating environment. Since these interactions are in rapid change, it is not enough to know how the organization itself functions, and not even how it interacts with its environment at the present moment in time: *one must also know how the interactions are likely to shape up in coming years.*

Such knowledge cannot be acquired by focusing on the structures and functions of the company itself, nor can it be obtained by extrapolating past trends into the future. Current trends are strongly nonlinear: they are likely to deflect, bifurcate, flourish, or vanish. Foreseeing their evolution requires acquaintance not only with the trends themselves (not even with the megatrends described by John Naisbitt);[2] they call for familiarity with the *dynamics* that underlies and drives the events that manifest the long-term system-evolving trends.

The Obsolescence of the Mainstream Approaches

The thesis we maintain in this book is that the sort of business knowledge of the first kind that is practiced in many companies has become obsolete, and business knowledge of the second kind, while more timely, is insufficient. Management concepts that were new in the first half of this century, and dominant throughout the postwar years, are now terminally outdated.

Consider the dominant kind of business knowledge of the first kind. As a carryover from nineteenth-century natural science, especially Newton's "classical mechanics," executives thought of their companies as complex mechanisms. They believed that the best way to run such mechanisms was by a rigorous hierarchical organization, controlled by those at the top. Top management was the sole possessor of information regarding the state and the objectives of the enterprise. It was an external controller, commanding all parts of the enterprise-machine without being commanded, or even particularly influenced, by its lower echelons. Power was highly concentrated, together with responsibility and overview; middle management had access only to such information as was immediately relevant to its task.

The distribution of tasks was established at headquarters: the company's functions were mechanistically divided into individual work components. The top people assigned the tasks and instructed everyone else to fulfill them. Employees were not to comment on the instructions, only to obey them. Motivation for task-fulfillment was to be created by material incentives bolstered by threats; individual creativity and initiative were considered unnecessary nuisance. In the machinelike enterprise, management was to be the sole source of ideas and knowledge—the sole driver.

Planning was based on a firm belief in control and predictability. Effects were traced to causes, and causes were quantitatively analyzed. Company operations based on cause-effect chains were given value independent of time and place: as in a machine, the same input was held always to produce the same output. Top management concentrated on transformation process: with the right input, the desired output would follow. This was the essence of mainstream management thinking during most of this century.

The mechanistic concept remained dominant for many decades: the economic growth environment of the postwar period did not provide grounds to question it. Executives could run their companies as if they were reliable machines, and could even engage in personal bravado; almost anything an enterprising manager would try had a knack of succeeding. There was no need to rethink basic concepts—if things get better and better on their own, why bother to look further than one's nose? There was no need to worry about whether there would be progress; it was enough to guess what shape it would take, and how one could benefit from it.

Management had tangible reasons for self-confidence. Technological progress seemed assured, and expanding markets seemed to distribute the benefits of growth. The postwar economy welcomed all entrepreneurs; they could grow as the economy expanded. Long-term costs, if any, were hidden in the long term. Businesspeople were fond of saying that there was no call to be concerned with the future. In the long term, as Keynes has said, we shall all be dead.

In the 1970s and 1980s, the situation had changed. The economic growth curve flattened out, optimistic extrapolations failed to come true. In their computerized world model, Jay Forrester and Dennis Meadows argued that growth has outer limits.[3] Social alienation and anomie rose, and technology produced unexpected side effects: scares and catastrophes at Three Mile Island, Bhopal, and Chernobyl; the ozone hole over the Antarctic; recurrent instances of acid rain and oil spill; and worsening environmental pollution in cities and on land. Belief in progress was shaken. Intellectuals and youth groups found it necessary, and some segments of society fashionable, to espouse the view that technological advance is dangerous and should be halted. As environmental effects and social value change were introduced as new factors in the equations of corporate success, managers, together with consultants and management theorists, began to reexamine their operative assumptions.

The failure of confidence in the dominant concept had solid reasons: in a rapidly changing environment, mechanistic thinking based on rigid and uniform causal chains is bound to produce shocks and surprises. As new technologies come rapidly on line, as markets become integrated and internationalized, as product cycles become shorter and product lines diversified, and as clients and consumers demand shorter delivery times and higher quality, a mechanistically run hierarchical enterprise is increasingly unable to cope. The centralization of information and its slow one-way penetration to lower echelons produce fatal mistakes—and then terminal rigidity.

Yet the concept of the company that persists in conservative circles today is still that of a mechanism that can be "driven" from above with a rationalization of tasks within a clear-cut matrix structure. But this is no longer functional. Frederick Taylor's "scientific management,"[4] designed to augment productivity by linking (originally through time-and-motion studies) each activity to a specific task and eliminating all time spent on coordination, communication, and other "nonproductive activities," has been overtaken by rapid and substantive changes in the operating environment.

By the last decade of this century, changes in the way leading companies conduct business have entirely outstripped the capacity of the Taylorian paradigm to produce satisfactory results. *Within* the corporation, the diffusion of information and the growth in the intensity and number of interfaces between people, departments, and divisions have changed how decisions are being made and productivity increases occur. In regard to the *outside* world, the boundary between the corporation and its environment has become fuzzy. The core activities of the enterprise are now frequently subcontracted, and networks of partnerships with other firms are becoming as intensive as internal organizational structures. Reliance on distributors and suppliers has become a key competitive success factor, and company linkage to local communities and ecologies is emerging as a new factor of corporate survival.

The Taylorian enterprise is not equipped for navigation in today's globalized and information-imbued seas. A different business knowledge is required. The new knowledge must:

• enable executives to cope with increasingly unpredictable economic conditions;

• offer sufficient flexibility to use new technologies as they come on line;

• enable the company to enter new fields of activity and leave old ones as opportunities present themselves; and

- be capable of keeping track of the growing interdependence of the enterprise with other enterprises and wider economic and social processes in the current, intensely information-penetrated and rapidly globalizing economic and financial environment.

The Search for Alternatives

Although mainstream management has been slow to change, for more than half a century front-line theorists have recognized the obsolescence of mechanistic concepts and shifted attention to nonconventional success factors. For example, Elton Mayo and Kurt Lewin have investigated the effect of leadership styles on human relations and drawn the consequences; Herbert Simon developed this method by relating management decisions to structures and processes within the organization, as well as to the objectives of managers. Then, in 1958, Jay Forrester published his *Harvard Business Review* article on dynamic feedback processes in industry.[5] Thereafter, the twilight of mechanistic management thinking deepened perceptibly.

Since the mid-1960s, sustained efforts have been made to view the enterprise on the level of the whole, with dynamic systems properties of its own.

- The dynamic systems approach has been embraced in the cybernetic school pioneered by W. Ross Ashby and Stafford Beer.
- The management theorists of the St. Gallen school in Switzerland, and of the Sloan School of Management at M.I.T., have been concentrating on interactions between decisions and structures in the attempt to integrate the enterprise as a whole.
- Russell Ackoff and colleagues at the University of Pennsylvania's Wharton School of Business in the United States, and Michael C. Jackson and collaborators in England, have been elaborating the dynamic systems concept by viewing the enterprise as a quasi-organic system embedded in a wide and complex social, ecological, and technological milieu.
- Tom Peters, one of the most widely read general management gurus, after having distilled recipes for "excellence" in the practice of successful companies, has come to advocate structural reforms and personal empowerment in a world of chaos and instability.
- Shoshana Zuboff, as well as Peter Keen, have been calling attention to the importance of new information technologies, changing cultures, and ecological processes in the management of the enterprise.
- George Stalk, Jr., and John Hout have been describing time-based processes that connect parts of the corporation to each other, as well as the corporation itself to its environment.

- Management experts have been borrowing concepts from engineering (Michael Hammer) as well as from architecture (David Nadler).

- Organization gurus have been concentrating on structures and processes within the organization itself; strategy consultants have been emphasizing the need to focus on competitive success factors and underlying economic levers to improve positioning; and technology consultants have been stressing the importance of research and development in both processes and products.

Looking Ahead, Not Back

The purpose of locating the required operative knowledge base is to enable managers to look forward and not back; to proact rather than just react; to anticipate trends rather than remain at their mercy. This purpose was not as important in the past, in a comparatively stable business environment. In the past, managers could hope to ensure continued success for their enterprise by studying its balance sheet. If it was satisfactory, the company's strategy worked and could be set forth; if it was unsatisfactory, the causes of the problem had to be identified in view of creating a suitably modified strategy. In the relatively high-growth environment of the postwar period, this kind of knowledge base sufficed, even if using it resembled driving on a highway while looking in the rearview mirror. As long as the road was straight and the way free, the view to the rear gave usable information for ongoing steering and acceleration. But when the road began to curve, managers found themselves in danger of driving their companies into the ditch.

Today, in the practice of leading-edge companies, "driving by the balance sheet" has been all but abandoned. Leading managers know that the future is not necessarily—and is not even likely to be—a direct continuation of the past. Another recipe for sustained success has supplemented the analysis of the balance sheet: "do everything to satisfy the customer." According to management consultants and quality circle advocates, the customer is king. In becoming customer-oriented, managers attempt to become flexible, to empower people, and to get their collaborators to work with the customers both singly and in teams. This is the concept that underlies today's much-touted TQM (total quality management). Here, products and services are to be continuously improved to drive defects out, put quality in, and satisfy the wishes and wants of the customer.

TQM is no doubt an improvement on driving by the balance sheet, since now management makes sure that the company is squarely on the road. But this is not enough. In an unstable business climate, driving by the current reality of the business environment is not a guarantee of keeping up with the *changes* that intervene in that environment. As long as the company had a market well in its grasp, continuous piecemeal improvement could help it to stay ahead of the competition. But hardly any company today has a market safely in its grasp. Competitive advantage, and therewith markets, change suddenly and discontinuously. In today's world, driving by TQM is like looking out the side window while barrelling down a curvy road. The needed adjustments to corporate strategy can only be effected at the last minute; and by then they are risky, costly, and difficult.

Not surprisingly, a 1993 survey by Arthur D. Little found that in the United States 93 percent of firms surveyed had TQM programs, but only 36 percent of the executives they polled regarded them as having a significant impact on their company's competitive position. This low level of confidence is by no means misplaced: while many (although not all) customers know what they want *today*, very few can anticipate what they will want *tomorrow*.

For example (to remain with the motoring metaphor), the trend toward more engine horsepower in automobiles over the *past* twenty years reflects the customer's desire for faster acceleration and higher top speed. This trend, however, is likely to reverse in the *next* twenty years. When city and highway traffic congestion reaches a critical point, when pollution levels move toward some critical threshold, and when fuel prices soar beyond economically and psychologically tolerable levels, the majority of customers will not want more horsepower and more speed: the importance of fuel economy will outweigh the importance of speed and power. Managers who rely on asking their customers will be blind to the sudden changes catalyzed when critical trends deflect. Those who are equipped with a realistic concept of the underlying trends, however, will be able to anticipate the changes: they will be in a position to make use of the intervening years to prepare their company for coping with them.

Sudden curves along the road require that managers look forward and take in the relevant contours of their business environment. Managerial vision must be foresightful and penetrating. A superficial view will identify only the symptoms of change, but not its causes—and hence not its likely course. Familiarity with the nature and role of information and communications technology, although needed, is not enough in itself. Effective corporate strategies of activity repositioning and organizational restructuring presuppose a sound knowledge not only of the current shape of the business environment (where the company is today), but also of its likely evolution (where the company must head to if it is to stay competitive).

Gary Hamel and C. K. Prahalad are correct when they say that the greatest competitive advantage a company can possess is a vision of the future.[6] This is even more valuable than a large bank account or a lean organization. Firms that possess future vision have a sense of purpose, can elicit deep commitment from their collaborators, and can avoid wasting time on useless experiments and dead ends.

Consultant Michael Annison found that all his consulting assignments over the past decades focused one way or another on three issues: What patterns and ideas underlie the changes we experience? What will the future look like? and How can we manage change?[7]

Scenario builders such as Peter Schwartz note (as he did in *The Art of the Long View*) that whenever one looks for the driving forces needed to create relevant scenarios of the future, one must consider society, technology, economics, and politics, as well as the environment.[8] In nearly every situation, forces from each of these areas make a crucial difference to the scenarios. That they do is the real reason why managers need to expand their current knowledge base.

But this reason does not in itself warrant staying with the technique of scenario building. Scenario theorists look further and wider than most other management theorists, yet their approach does not entirely fill the bill. The currently created scenarios operate mostly on the surface; they do not penetrate into the moving forces behind the scenes. Current scenarios are event-driven—they do not disclose the dynamics that *generate* the events. This can lead to misleading results. As Charles Handy points out in *The Age of Unreason*, the future could be anything, but it will not be a linear continuation of the past.[9]

ACCESSING BUSINESS KNOWLEDGE OF THE THIRD KIND

Envisaging alternative futures helps managers muster flexibility to cope with the kinds of changes that are actually taking place, but it cannot assure them that these are the kinds of changes that will continue to occur in the future. To anticipate the kinds of changes that are likely to come about in the foreseeable future, managers need business knowledge of the third kind. This, as Figure 1.1 illustrates, is knowledge that enables managers to obtain a meaningful view of the complex processes that affect—and often buffet—their enterprise.

Foresighted knowledge is not just efficient: in the long term, it may be the key to survival. This is because the struggle for corporate survival will intensify in coming years, and hence the competitive edge will become more and more crucial. Today there is already accelerating attrition among competitors in every sector of industry. In some cases, such as the automobile industry, the logic of consolidation is driven by global economies of scale and experience, and this leads to intense competition among world-class players. In the ensuing battle of giants, a competitive edge by one or another is likely to prove decisive. In other cases, for example, in the international airline industry, growing competition cre-

Figure 1.1
Evolution of the Working Knowledge of Managers

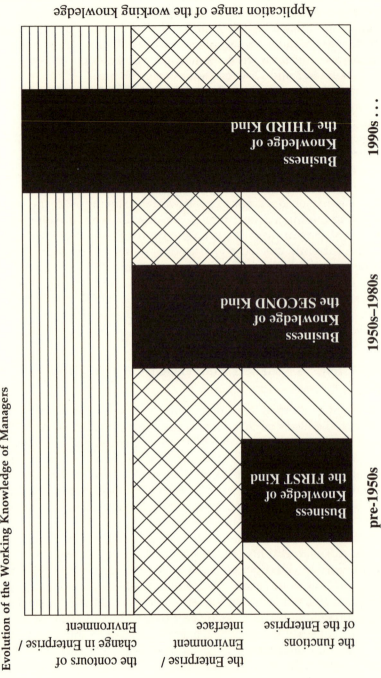

Application range of the working knowledge

Business
Knowledge of
the THIRD Kind

Business
Knowledge of
the SECOND Kind

Business
Knowledge of
the FIRST Kind

1990s ...

1950s–1980s

pre-1950s

the contours of
change in Enterprise /
Environment

the Enterprise /
Environment
interface

the functions
of the Enterprise

ates the kind of natural selection where only the most adaptive and quick-on-the-draw survive. In every sector and every industry, the players that compete best will not be the wealthiest and the most powerful, but rather the most flexible and the most insightful.

This third kind of business knowledge exists, and it can be acquired. To acquire it, executives must know *where* it is developed, and *how* they can gain access to it. We provide some pointers here.

"Third-kind knowledge" comes from the sciences. To be sure, it does *not* come from the mechanistic sciences of the 1920s that were the inspiration of Taylor's "scientific management" theory. The new knowledge comes from the new sciences—from the emerging disciplines that develop the current theories of chaos, of dissipative structures, of complex dynamical systems, and of biological as well as cosmological evolution.

The new sciences show how complex systems coevolve with their environments. Applied to the business sphere, they elucidate how this coevolution affects individuals within their activity domains, and how individuals and their activities affect the developmental dynamics of their organization.

Recourse to scientific insight is needed because the evolution of complex systems is not ordinarily apparent even to those who evolve the systems. This is nothing unusual—it is so throughout nature. The individual growth of plants and behavior of animals determine the way their ecology evolves, but the individual organisms have no knowledge of the developmental paths opened up by them. Also, the cells in our brain drive the processes that underlie our consciousness, yet the brain cells know nothing of the purposes we entertain in our conscious mind. In the same way, managers, collaborators, clients, and competitors develop organizations and markets without necessarily knowing the nature of the evolution they produce.

To be an effective manager, it is not enough to *create* change—one must also know how one's actions impact on the developmental dynamics of the organization he or she is dealing with.

A grasp of the interactive dynamics that drives organizations in the contemporary world is not a mere appendage to the concepts managers already possess regarding their company and its industry sector. Knowledge of the third kind partly replaces, partly colors and shapes, knowledge of the previous kinds. The company, its industry, its information technology (IT) platform, and its social and ecological environment appear in a new light. The organization is no longer viewed as a vast mechanism, divisible to component parts that are controllable by unchanging rules. Instead it is seen as an organic system embedded in its environment, with its own evolutionary trajectory, and an intrinsic capability for self-organization in interaction with the world around it. To factor in the interactive evolutionary process has become essential for effective and responsible management. It replaces reliance on personal intuition as a basis for strategic decisions.

The evolutionary principles outlined in this book make use of the interactive dynamics discovered in the new evolutionary sciences to create up-to-date guidelines for effective management. They help managers navigate their enterprise through periods of turbulence to higher plateaus of productivity and dynamism.

The successful managers of the twenty-first century will be those that forget the obsolete elements of the mainstream knowledge of twentieth-century management and replace them with the evolutionary principles required for the next-century management of complex systems. They will possess the crucial *insight edge*.

NOTES

1. Shoshana Zuboff, *In the Age of the Smart Machine* (New York: Basic Books, 1988), p. 243.

2. John Naisbitt, *Megatrends: Ten New Directions Transforming Our Lives* (New York: Warner Books, 1982).

3. Donella Meadows and Dennis Meadows et al., *The Limits to Growth* (Washington, D.C.: Universe Books, 1972).

4. W. F. Taylor, *Scientific Shoveling* (n.p., 1911). See also F. Gilbreth, *Bricklaying Systems* (New York: Clark, 1909) and W. Leffingwell, *Office Management: Principles and Practice* (n.p.: Shaw Co., 1925). For a more modern introduction to the subject, see D. Nelson, *Frederick W. Taylor and the Rise of Scientific Management* (Madison: University of Wisconsin Press, 1980).

5. J. W. Forrester, "Industrial Dynamics: A Major Breakthrough for Decision-Makers," *Harvard Business Review* (1958): 37–66.

6. G. Hamel and C. K. Prahalad, "Corporate Imagination and Expeditionary Marketing," *Harvard Business Review* (July/August 1991).

7. Michael Annison, *Managing the Whirlwind* (Englewood, Colo.: Medical Group Management Association, 1993).

8. Peter Schwartz, *The Art of the Long View: The Path to Strategic Insights for Yourself & Your Company* (New York: Doubleday & Co., 1991).

9. Charles Handy, *The Age of Unreason* (Cambridge, Mass.: Harvard Business School Press, 1991).

Chapter 2

The Evolutionary Gigatrend (EGT)

To navigate without a compass is always risky, even when one has a good sense of the sea. On today's turbulent seas everyday details can still be left to business acumen and to technical skills, but strategic decisions cannot—they must be properly informed. At the dawn of the twenty-first century, this calls for acquiring the basic minimum of evolutionary literacy: familiarity with the fundamental logic of change in our rapidly evolving socio-technological world.

Evolutionary literacy is a necessary foundation for competence in the management of contemporary businesses. This is because today's companies are increasingly linked with the society in which they operate, as well as with their environment. Consequently, the trends that shape these larger systems are key points of reference in the reliable and responsible management of our highly interlinked enterprises.

But just what is evolutionary literacy? As a first approximation, we can define evolutionary literacy as acquaintance with the dynamics of the systems that make up the pertinent environment of business and society. These systems fit one next to, and often into, the other: they are families, communities, groups, organizations, enterprises, towns, cities and states, and the system of ecologies ranging from the ecosystem of the local pond to the intercontinental ecosystem spanning the globe. Typically, the dynamics of these systems are exhibited on the level of the whole system, and not (or not necessarily) on the level of the parts. This, however, would oblige us to look for elucidation at the planet-wide socio-ecosystem as a whole. We would have a problem on our hands: the evolution of that system, made up of all humans, human societies, and other systems in nature, cannot be seen in every detail—the largest Cray supercomputer could not cope with the myriad reactions and interactions that go on inside it. But the problem is not insurmountable. Using the concepts of the new sciences of systems and of evolution, we can see the system-wide processes in basic outline. While seeing this calls for some level of simplification, it need not occur at the expense of substance. This is because we can now make use of an appropriate form of simplification: to map the whole system in terms of its own dynamics. (This contrasts with the classical method, which was to ignore the whole and concentrate on the part. That method threw out the baby with the bath water: as noted in Chapter 1, the basic dynamics of a system often appear only on the level of the whole.) With the new method, the key factors are represented, so that loss of detail does not entail loss of substance. Quite the contrary: the grasp of the whole system's characteristic dynamics helps us to classify and order higher-resolution details. Additional data fall into place; they illustrate and explicate the relevant features of the dynamics that characterize the whole.

Seeing the dynamics of the whole system is important, because this gives us a clue to the dynamics that drive fundamental transformations even in the smaller-scale systems that populate the world around us. Hence we shall not hesitate to raise our eyes to look at the dynamics that hallmark the whole system that has evolved, and continues to evolve, on this planet. This means looking at the long-term system-wide transformation processes that embrace both nature and society, in history as well as today. (For the sake of convenience, we shall henceforth refer to this trend as the "evolutionary gigatrend," or EGT for short. Here, *giga* means "giant," *mega* means "great.")

An evolutionary gigatrend is far more basic and decisive than any trend currently known to managers and economists, including the megatrends popularized by John Naisbitt in the 1980s. But does the EGT truly exist? There is good reason to believe that it does: there is now considerable literature on it, including a widely translated and reprinted treatise produced by one of the present authors (Ervin Laszlo, *Evolution: The General Theory*, rev. ed. [Crestkill, NJ: Hampton Press, 1996]).

THE DRIVERS OF THE EGT

The characteristic features that hallmark the evolution of systemic processes in our world can be grasped under the heading of a few key concepts. These concepts have equivalent technical definitions in the physical and in the life sciences, but here our interest focuses on concepts that pertain to the human world. We thus group the fundamental concepts under basic and relatively simple categories and outline their relevance to the manager entrusted with navigation in today's rapidly evolving business-cum-social-cum-ecological world.

The First Driver: Technological Change and Innovation

Innovation of a kind that affects the way people live and work is conceptual innovation linked with practical applications. In the modern world, it is *technological* innovation, directly or indirectly based on advances in science. Such innovation has a major impact on society—an impact that is generally irreversible. Effective technological change is always one-way: it is from the hoe to the plow, and not the other way around. Even if many technical procedures are invented, only those that represent an improvement in the effectiveness or efficiency of some procedure are actually adopted and diffused. This kind of improvement can be transcended, but it cannot be forgotten. The irreversibility of technological change has held true throughout history, from the hoe to the plow, and from the steam engine to the jet airplane. It holds true today as we innovate fiber optics, solar cells, integrated circuits, and lasertronics.

The technologies of the Stone Age were limited to kindling and to some extent controlling fire, and to making and using tools such as the axe, the dagger, and various other tools for cutting and scraping. When *Homo erectus* evolved into *sapiens*, new technologies were developed, making more effective use of the human hand with its counterposed thumb. Tool use expanded from drilling, scraping, threading, and cutting, to twisting, grinding, and pressure flaking, with raw materials that included bone, ivory, and antler in addition to stone, wood, and skin.

With the advent of the Neolithic Age some 8,000 to 10,000 years ago, additional tools were invented, such as hammers with a hole for handles, and saws, daggers, knives, and sickles. They were further improved by gouging, carving, polishing, and grinding. In the course of time, more durable agricultural tools were developed, made of metal: first copper, then bronze, and then iron.

Except for reliance on steel rather than iron, the 8,000 years that separated the Neolithic from the Industrial Age witnessed relatively few changes in basic agricultural tools; the sickle, the hoe, the chisel, the saw, the hammer, and the knife continued in use. Real changes occurred mainly in regard to new techniques of irrigation and the introduction of new plant varieties. Then, in the nineteenth century, the Industrial Revolution brought a battery of new technologies on the scene, led by the newly discovered power of steam. It shifted the focus of development from agriculture to industry.

The first industrial breakthroughs occurred in textiles. Innovations in spinning cotton stimulated a chain of related inventions which led to the emergence of machines capable of factory-based mass production. Industrial development spread from textiles to iron, as cheaper cast iron replaced more expensive wrought iron. Closely on the heel of innovations in the machine tool industry were developments in the chemical industry. By the middle of the nineteenth century, Britain was a major manufacturing power, followed closely by Germany, France, and the United States. Western societies transformed from an agricultural to an industrial mold.

Many of the great technological inventions that spawned the automobile, steel, cement, petrochemical, and pharmaceutical industries took place in the late nineteenth century. With few exceptions, the steel mills built since World War II are based on the Bessemer steel process developed in the 1860s; the rotary kiln, patented by Fredrick Ransome in 1885, is used in today's cement production; the synthetic dyes of that period were basic to the development of modern chemical industries. The traction-based combustion engine, a key innovation in modern transportation, appeared in the 1880s on the heels of Edison's electric light bulb, and was followed by Marconi's wireless and the Wright brothers' flying machine. Such innovations transformed industrial production, shifting it from coal and steam, textiles, machine tools, glass, pre-Bessemer forged steel, and labor-intensive agriculture, to electricity, the internal combustion engine, organic chemicals, and large-scale manufacturing. A prodigious number of scientific and technological breakthroughs joined with practical industrial applications laid the groundwork for the twentieth-century expansion of business firms from local artisanal workshops to globe-spanning manufacturing empires.

Then, in the second half of the twentieth century, a new type of technological change occurred, replacing reliance on massive energy and raw material inputs with the more intangible resource known as information. A growing quantity of information has come to be stored on optical discs, communicated by fiber optics, and processed by computers governed by sophisticated programs with millions of operations per second. The diffusion of information into the workplace has been the defining innovation of the late twentieth century, leading to fundamental changes in the locus and exercise of power, the measurement and control of productivity, and the complexity of intrafirm as well as interfirm relations. The world of business has become informationalized and interlinked, and launched irreversibly on the path to globalization.

The Second Driver: Complexity and Convergence

Some two centuries ago, the first industrial revolution started out with the steam engine, the winning of iron from coke, and the weaving of textiles. It could be successfully run by enterprises headed by one man and owned by one family. By the middle of the nineteenth century, the revolution spread to embrace the making of steel, and the use of steel, iron, and the steam engine in railroads and steamships on globe-spanning trade routes. This led to a vast expansion of national markets, and larger and more complex organizational structures had to be developed to effectively exploit the enlarged economies of scale. In the course of the twentieth century, electric power, the combustion engine, and the use of batch chemical elements called for still more sophisticated organizational structures to translate the fruits of R&D into profitable ventures in highly diversified product lines. The latest technologies link science and technology with production, marketing, services, and they impel once again the reorganization of the structures and procedures of the enterprises using them.

The trend toward complexity is now evident in every sphere of life and experience; organizations, networks, ways of life, jobs, as well as states and communities all have become progressively more complex. Convergence is a less visible factor of contemporary life, but it is just as real. It is evident in the way smaller-size units come together in larger systems, and the way the larger systems themselves integrate in still more embracing mega-systems. This process, too, cuts across all spheres of experience, occurring in the private sphere as well as in the public.

Complexity and convergence are distinct factors in the evolution of the complex system made up of society and nature, but they are not independent of the other factors. Indeed, we can readily understand how the ongoing stream of technological change and innovation complexifies the technology-imbued systems that come about, and networks them into ever larger units. (In the language of science, we can say that technological innovation accesses and converts more and more of the free energy available in the biosphere, and this additional input of effectively utilized energy "drives" the evolution of human, artificial, and natural systems. This is because systems exposed to a flow of free energy inevitably gain in structure and complexity—as we discuss in more detail in the Appendix at the end of the volume.)

Convergence follows logically after complexification. This is because there are limits to the complexity that any system can tolerate; if it oversteps these, it loses internal coherence, and also its ties with the external environment become nonfunctional. Sooner or later, an overly complex system must disappear—disaggregate to those of its elements that did not overstep their own limits of complexity. If a complex system is to continue functioning, it must structure both itself and its relations with its relevant environment. Internally, it must create levels of organization that coordinate and control (in a cybernetic, guidance sense) the already existing levels—this is required to maintain coherence. Externally, the system must evolve mutually constructive ties with other systems in its environment. These ties lead then to the creation of a higher-level system (or systems), in which the given system is a functional part. This yields the process of convergence.

Put concisely, convergence is the progressive coordination of previously semi-independent (but then increasingly interlocking) systems within higher level structures.

In the course of recorded history, convergence has brought together tribes, clans, villages, and provinces in more and more extensive, complex, and diversified social, political, and economic systems. The archaic empires of China and India incorporated and coordinated villages and regional communities in subcontinental administrative structures; the classical Roman Empire was built of numerous city-states, regions, and provinces under the rule of Pax Romana; and the colonial empires of Europe consisted not only of villages, towns, and provinces in the mother countries but also of strings of overseas colonies.

The process of economic and political convergence is continuing in our day. In the *public sphere*, its advanced expressions are the intensifying ties between states on the continental or subcontinental level. The European Union, the North American Free Trade Agreement, the Association of South East Asian Nations, and the Asia and Pacific Economic Community are but the tip of an iceberg of more than four dozen regional communities that operate, struggle to operate, or are envisaged to operate on all continents. As they evolve, they create the necessary basis for a further stage of public-sector convergence—a stage where it will unfold on the inter*regional* (rather than on the inter*national*) level. This stage of convergence will bring together entire economic communities with global-level accords. The Uruguay Round of GATT (the General Agreement on Tariffs and Trade), where the crucial negotiations involved the United States and the group of states that make up the European Union, is an advance indicator of comprehensive systemic arrangements on the interregional economic, and ultimately also social and political, level of organization.

In the *private sector*, convergence brings together enterprises within increasingly complex multiproduct and multinational structures. The visible result of this process is the global corporation, with its network-like branches operating in a growing variety of industry branches on an increasing number of geographic markets.

The continuation of business-world convergence now pitches the global players against each other. This is producing further mergers, fusions, and acquisitions, and other more innovative forms of functional linkages. They interface partners and former competitors within ever more embracing industry giants, flexibly linking their own increasingly autonomous subsidiaries.

There is progressive concentration among the successful global players themselves: the most competitive giants corner more and more of the market. This is accompanied by attrition among the less competitive

Figure 2.1
The Enterprise and Its Environing Systems

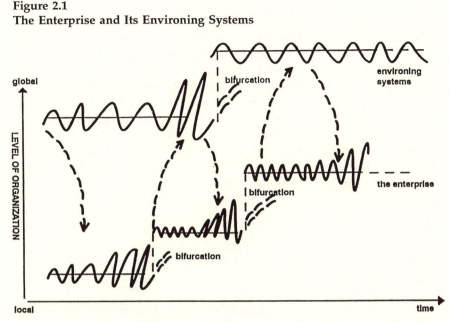

The enterprise and its environing social, natural, and business systems constantly interact, at times buffering and at other times intensifying each other's instabilities. Stability in one system creates stability in others; conversely, critical instability catalyzes corresponding instabilities and leads to bifurcations. As a result, enterprise and environment coevolve to ever more complex, embracing, and higher-level orders.

firms. In the United States, it is often four or five companies that control 80 percent of a market sector. In Japan, 80 percent market share is frequently reached by less than four. And in Europe, where each country has historically protected its industry leaders, the post-1992 single market with its reduced trade barriers is leading to a rapid concentration of competitors, partly through attrition and partly through mergers and acquisitions. In the food industry, for example, there are 250 companies in Europe with sales in excess of 200 million Ecu (the European accounting unit), but industry analysts predict that by 1998 there will not be more than 100 such companies. The survivors are likely to prosper: their sales may increase to over 20 billion Ecu (and then Euro) and reach the level of the U.S.-based food giants, with whom they will compete on both regional and global markets.

As a consequence of private sector convergence, corporate competition moves to ever higher organizational levels. It is beginning to be played out today at the tip of a complex pyramid where less than a dozen giant network players confront each other in practically all existing and emerging markets.

The Third Driver: Bifurcation and Chaos

The evolutionary path of complex systems is seldom smooth and continuous. This fact was recognized by theoretical scientists for decades, but it was only with the wider availability of high-speed computers in the last few years that the process could be understood with mathematical precision. The evolutionary paths are hallmarked by so-called "attractors" that define the time sequence (the specific pattern) traced by the states of a system as it pursues an evolutionary trajectory. There are several varieties of attractors: stable point attractors, represented by an equilibrium point on the phase chart toward which the system tends; periodic attractors, which define cyclically recurring system states; and "strange" or "chaotic" attractors that model complex and not fully predictable system states.

When a complex system shifts from one set of attractors to others, its trajectory forks off into a new pattern. The term "bifurcation" describes this pattern shift. Depending on whether the shift is smooth and continuous, sudden, or discontinuous, the bifurcations are described as "subtle," "catastrophic," or "explosive."

In the new conception, systems in the real world evolve from a particular initial state along a trajectory of states until a pattern emerges in which the trajectory remains temporarily or permanently trapped. If the pattern shows that the evolution of the system comes to a rest, the process is governed by static attractors. If the pattern consists of a cycle with a definite periodicity, the evolution of the system is under the sway of periodic attractors. And if the sequence of system states comes neither to rest nor exhibits periodicity but becomes erratic, it is under the influence of strange or chaotic attractors.

Chaotic attractors are more widespread than previously believed: erratic behavior has been discovered in a great variety of systems. An entire discipline within mathematical system theory is now devoted to their study: this is the research specialty that became popularly known as "chaos theory." Despite its name, the theory eliminates rather than discovers chaos—the processes it studies only appear chaotic; on closer analysis they turn out to have a complex order of their own. As Figure 2.2 shows, seemingly unordered systems yield to analysis by the strange yet ordered shapes of chaotic or strange attractors. These include the Lorenz butterfly, the Birkhof and the Shaw bagel, the Rössler band and the Rössler funnel, among many others (the above systems have been named after their discoverers and the geometrical shape of the attractors).

Contemporary chaos theory reduces chaos to complex order in processes as varied as fluids in a flow and the blending of substances during solidification. Turbulence in gases and liquids, for example, has been

Figure 2.2
Representations in Chaos-Theory Models of Real-World Systems

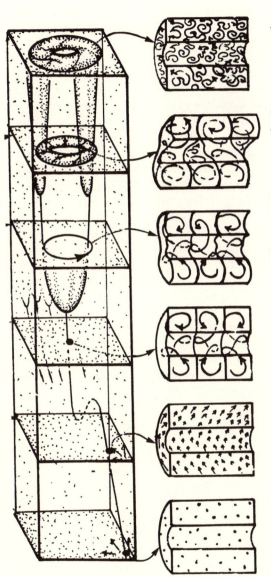

Representations in chaos-theory models of real-world systems exhibit order where a "snapshot"-type representation would only show chaos. Above: the movement of a liquid in a spherical container. Each cutaway snapshot of the container corresponds to one "phase-portrait" showing the evolution of the attractors. (The point-attractor shows imaginary ink drops in the liquid at rest. As the point-attractor evolves, more complex movement is registered in the container, until the movement becomes entirely chaotic [on the right].) Courtesy Ralph Abraham and C. Shaw, *Dynamics: The Geometry of Behavior* (Santa Cruz, Calif.: Aeriel Press, 1984).

known since the nineteenth century, but has not been well understood. By 1923, experiments in fluid dynamics demonstrated that annular Taylor vortices appear when stirring increases beyond a critical point; beyond that point further stirring produces abrupt transformations in the liquid and ultimately turbulence. Currently turbulence is modelled by chaotic attractors and is shown to exhibit the complex varieties of order typical of all chaotic systems.

Order of extreme sensitivity, due to the presence of multiple loops and feedbacks in systems, has been discovered in more and more areas of investigation. The healthy nervous system, for example, exhibits such order: it includes multiple domains of chaos. A loss of chaotic properties entails diseases like depression and epilepsy. It seems that chaotic states are information-rich, whereas regular, nonchaotic states are monotonous and have little flexibility. Our heart, too, beats in a manner typical of chaotic systems, fluctuating considerably even in normal conditions and at rest. Such strange patterns as ventricular fibrillation appear entirely regular when interpreted as a manifestation of an underlying chaotic state.

Many natural systems are permanently in a state of chaos: the world's weather is a good example. The weather system is subject to myriad tiny fluctuations, each of which can produce a cascade of changes that influences the overall weather pattern. According to a now legendary account of the so-called "butterfly effect" (which was really named after the butterfly-like shape of a strange attractor—shown here in Figure 2.3—first discovered in the 1960s by American meteorologist Edward Lorenz as he attempted to model world weather patterns on the computer), a butterfly flapping its wings in California creates a minute air turbulence that can end up creating a storm in Outer Mongolia.

Chaotic phenomena also crop up in the business world. For example, the relationship between a firm's profits and the size of its advertising budget exhibits irregular cyclic characteristics typical of chaotic systems. As spending on advertising rises, total profits first tend to increase (the revenue effect) but tend to level off and finally to decline (as increasing expenditures eat into profits). This prompts managers to reduce the advertising budget, which then raises net profits in the following period. Higher net profits allow an increase in the advertising outlay which leads, in turn, to a further increase in profits. Then the phenomenon of declining profits reappears. The cycle can repeat ad infinitum. It neither converges to a stable equilibrium point nor falls into a predictably repeating pattern. Such cycles, which repeat with unpredictable oscillations, cannot be modelled with the classical mathematical tools; they require dynamical systems modelling by chaotic attractors. (More on this in the Appendix at the end of this volume.)

As we shall see, the transformation of entire organizational structures provides even more significant examples requiring the use of chaos-

Figure 2.3
Butterfly-Shaped Computer Model of Air Currents

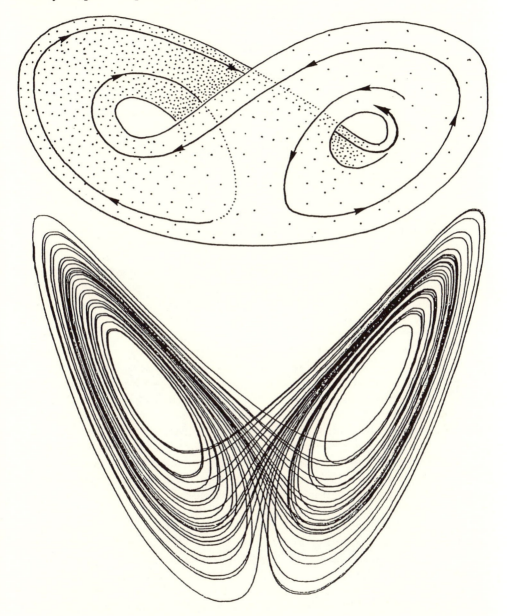

The vaguely butterfly-shaped computer model of air currents in the atmosphere discovered by meteorologist Edward Lorenz, to which this attractor owes its name (above), and a more recent computer-drawn butterfly attractor (below). The trajectory of system-states in these "phase-portraits" is highly sensitive: the smallest perturbation can flip the system from one wing of the butterfly to the other.

theoretical concepts. So-called "catastrophic bifurcations" are especially relevant for business companies: they show how a complex system moves from a chaotic condition to a newly ordered state through the reconfiguration of its internal forces and tensions. The chaos that intervenes in such transformations does not imply randomness even if the cycles fail to settle into a predictable pattern: chaotic attractors permit a range of random variations within their specific dynamic envelope.

Chaos theory and bifurcation dynamics are important additions to classical economic theories; their sophisticated conceptual and mathematical instruments can overcome the limitations of the classical concepts and tools. The new conceptual innovations offer a clearer understanding of what happens, can happen, and can be made to happen in a time of mounting social, political, economic, and environmental crises and transformations.

The Joint Effect of the Drivers: The Global System

In society, as in nature, the evolutionary dynamics creates an irreversible process. The biosphere is filling with biological species within increasingly complex and interacting ecologies; the human world, in turn, is filling with communities that exploit practically all the habitable environment and also exploit (or attempt to exploit) all the energies and raw materials that are technologically accessible to them. This process works like a rachet: it pulls both ecologies and societies to progressively higher levels of organization. As the overview offered in Figure 2.4 suggests, in the course of history Neolithic kinship-based hunting-gathering tribes gave rise to communal settlements, and then to agrarian-pastoral societies. These evolved into the archaic empires of Mesopotamia, Egypt, Persia, India, and China; and while some of these empires disappeared in the course of centuries, others survived through appropriate modifications of structure and process. In Europe, the fall of the Roman Empire led to a mosaic of feudal kingdoms and princedoms, and out of these basic units modern nation-states have evolved.

The present global socioeconomic/ecologic system has emerged in turn from the convergence of nation-states. Although it is significantly divorced from its natural milieu, this informationalized and globalized system continues to rely on the constant flow of energy that streams from the sun to the earth. The essential elements of the process are illustrated in Figure 2.5. Solar energy travels at the extremely high temperature of 5,600° (on the Kelvin scale); it reaches the earth's atmosphere at 260°K, and here on the surface it is in part converted into green leaves by the vegetation cover of the planet. Plant matter is further converted into both plant and animal biomass in the vast network of the biosphere's food chain. At each point of conversion, heat is generated, and waste-heat is radiated into the surroundings. The sum total of radiated heat, including

Figure 2.4
Progression of Organizational Levels

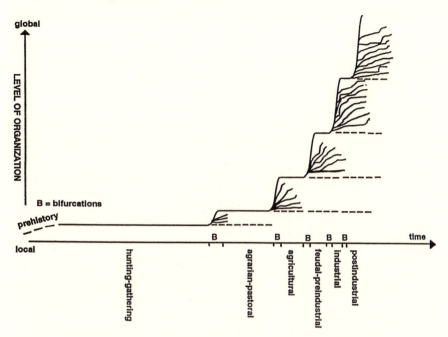

Throughout the span of recorded history, human societies have advanced to progressively higher organizational levels. The process began with the hunting-gathering tribes of the Stone Age and currently culminates in the coming of postindustrial societies globally integrated in the emerging information age. Each bifurcation, driven mainly by the widespread adoption of basic technological innovations, has impelled societies to more complex, more embracing levels of organization. Today, the widespread adoption of the new information and communication technologies drives the process to the global level.

the solar heat reflected from barren land surfaces and the oceans, leaves the earth for interplanetary space. Space, in our solar system as well as elsewhere in the cosmos, is a cool 2.7°K (this is the so-called cosmic background radiation, the remnant of the originally superhot "big bang" that gave birth to the universe). The difference between the 260°K energy source and the 2.7°K energy sink drives the cycles that maintain the global system with all the generative and regenerative processes essential to plant, animal, and human life.

THE EGT AND THE FUTURE

The drivers of the evolutionary gigatrend held sway in the growth and development of human societies throughout the span of recorded history. In the course of the twentieth century, the evolutionary process

Figure 2.5
The Biosphere

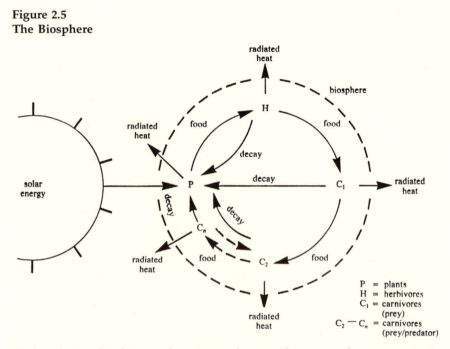

The biosphere is closed in regard to matter and open with respect to the energy streaming from the sun and radiating into surrounding space. The heat difference between the free energy reaching the earth from the sun and the waste energy radiated into space drives all irreversible processes on the surface of this planet. These processes configure and reconfigure matter into increasingly complex systems, starting with the conversion of solar energy into biomass by the green plant and culminating in the complex, free energy–driven cycles of vast ecosystems.

had accelerated, and at the end of this century it became vertiginous. The transition from classical industrial society to an information-imbued and increasingly globalized socioeconomic and ecologic system is now unfolding through an accelerated alternation of order and turbulence. In the past, this dynamic was reasonably under control. The changes and transformations due to the destabilization of a given type of social and economic structure were followed by technologically orchestrated leaps to renewed stability at a higher level of organization. These were the processes that dominated our evolution in the past. Can we rely on them to ensure our continued evolution in the future?

We cannot give an assured "yes" to this question. The evolutionary process has never been free of errors; however, in the past the errors could be locally contained. As their milieu degenerated—through defor- estation and soil erosion—agrarian and agricultural people migrated to greener pastures, or found new ways of compensating for the man/

nature disequilibria they have triggered. Technological progress could often create new equilibria (in modern agriculture, for example, through inputs of fertilizers and new crop varieties), enabling societies to replace reliance on earlier natural balances with technologically boosted generative cycles.

By contrast, in today's world, human impact on nature is planet-wide. Some of the most basic cycles of the biosphere's life-support systems are being impaired. If they become destabilized, we shall have to adapt to radically changed conditions. Given a population of close to six billion people, living for the most part at or near subsistence level, there is little room for error in this globalized system; even minor mistakes could induce regional ecodisasters or catastrophes, with population collapses of conceivably staggering dimensions.

Yet evolution, as we have noted, is not fate: alternative outcomes are always possible. The basic alternatives are evolution and extinction. Between them, there are many pathways of more or less successful evolution, and more or less total extinction. Technological innovation, for example, could bring unimaginable comfort and luxury to more people, or it could saw off the branch on which it is growing by overexploiting its resource base and thus impairing humanity's life-support systems. Complexity could lead to higher levels of coordination in flexible structures that serve the human interest, or it could produce hierarchical structures that suppress creativity and enslave freedom. Bifurcations produce transient chaos—windows to radically new conditions—and the new conditions could be better for humans than those that went before, or they could be worse. Humanity could be heading for a globally linked and informationalized world that is inhuman, repressive, and resource depleted, or it could be progressing to a global information society capable of offering optimum freedom of initiative and individual choice within a richly textured system of energies, resources, and natural regenerative cycles. The choice is ours—within its limits, the evolutionary gigatrend is permissive.

Working with the trend and making use of the beneficial opportunities it offers, or working in ignorance of it and perhaps at cross-purposes with it, is the choice that faces today's managers. Their responsibility for their company is inextricably bound up with responsibility for the systems within which their company operates—systems that are in turn an integral part of the human socio-ecological system of the planet.

In decision-making positions, evolutionary literacy has become just as vital as basic literacy in other jobs. It provides the insight that gives the edge in strategic decisions—the crucial edge for corporate success, as well as for sustained social and environmental livability.

Chapter 3

Shifting the Paradigm

The contemporary world is evolving from the industrial toward the post-industrial mold. This evolution calls for a corresponding shift in the thinking of managers. A postindustrial society is a knowledge society: in the context of such a society, the crucial factor is not access to natural resources, and not even access to unlimited capital—it is access to up-to-date knowledge and its transformation into products and services.

In the Industrial Age, manufacturing companies relied on a seemingly endless supply of raw material and cheap energy. Their aim was to produce mass-manufactured goods for mass markets. Managers created trade, advertising, and transport mechanisms to bridge the distance between producers and consumers and to place larger amounts of mass-produced goods on more markets. Power and wealth were linked to the accumulation of capital, the creation of raw material monopolies, the control of energy, the economies of scale, and the domination of mass markets.

This type of company has been disappearing in the advanced economies of the world. In its place is the postindustrial enterprise keyed to optimizing quality rather than quantity by increasing the information content of products and reducing their energy and raw material content. In the postindustrial company the knowledge frontier is the market, and the time value of transportation activities—and not the classical price mechanism—is the key to productivity. Managers reach customers through flexible, custom-tailored production methods, using innovative and customer-driven processes to link each activity in the delivery chain. Emphasis is on creativity and flexibility, and not on the rigid professionalism that dominated the classical industrial company.

STAGES AND DIMENSIONS OF ENTERPRISE EVOLUTION

The modern enterprise did not emerge complete in every detail, like Venus from the sea: it is itself a product of growth and evolution. Enterprise evolution does not necessarily follow the evolution of society, although it is obviously influenced by it. Enterprises are systems that have their own stages of development. These resemble the phases of birth, infancy, childhood, adolescence, and maturity in human beings. (Since enterprises can continuously renew themselves, they do not have the terminal stage of senescence typical of multicellular organisms.)

For all practical intents and purposes, it is sufficient to distinguish three major stages in the evolution of the enterprise: the initial, the developmental, and the systemic stages (see Figure 3.1).

The first stage in enterprise evolution corresponds to its infancy: it is the *initial stage*. The second stage follows as the enterprise grows larger and more complex. It grows out of its original framework and requires a more effective organizational structure than its founders' abilities and values can provide. This is the *developmental stage*. The third stage brings the enterprise to the form in which it can function in today's globalized and informationalized business environment: it is the mature *systemic stage*.

Unless the enterprise is created *ex nihilo* by an existing systemic mother company, it is started typically as a one-product or one-service company, established by one person, a family, or a small set of partners. It displays characteristics imposed on it by its founders. It is aggressive and competitive or adaptive and nonassertive; it is contented with its local niche and unwilling to move beyond it, or it is aggressively expansion- and growth-oriented. The personality of the founder can be in the foreground, as a charismatic leader and role model, or (more seldom) it can function behind the scenes, allowing collaborators and customers to shape the way the enterprise views itself and the face it presents to the outside world.

But once the enterprise is operative, the evolutionary gigatrend shapes its further development. The key aspects of this process are shown in Figure 3.2. Sustained competitiveness and productivity require that the structure of the initial stage be further elaborated. This is the case because larger markets, new competitors, evolving customer needs, and increasingly sophisticated technologies call for restructuring the enterprise's organizational structure. Inevitably, it grows beyond the mold first imposed on it by its founders.

In the developmental stage, the perhaps insightful and charismatic (but inescapably personality-bound) leadership of the initial stage is replaced by established principles and rules. These are embedded in a

Figure 3.1
Evolution of the Enterprise

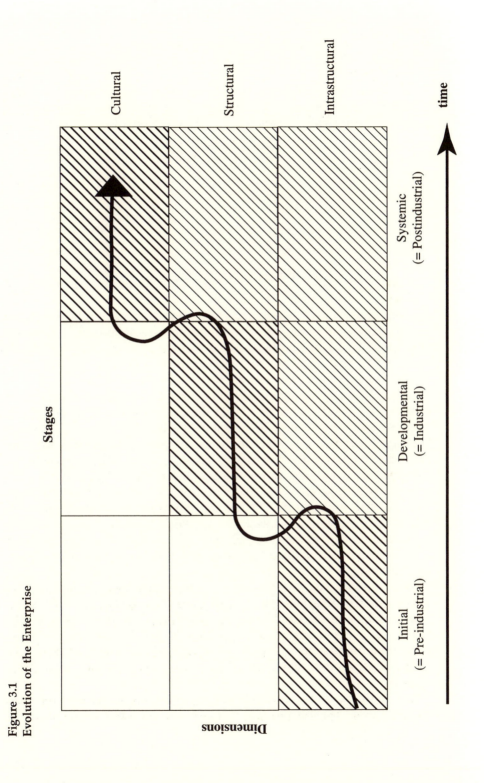

Figure 3.2
Evolution of the Global Enterprise (Key Dimensions)

ONE–PRODUCT FAMILY MANAGEMENT LOCAL ECONOMY		(time)			MULTI–LINE MULTI–DIVISION GLOBAL ECONOMY
operations	operations	operations	operations	operations	operations
	metrics	metrics	metrics	metrics	metrics
		competitors/ suppliers/ distributors	competitors/ suppliers/ distributors	competitors/ suppliers/ distributors	competitors suppliers/ distributors
			organization/ values	organization/ values	organization/ values
				alliances/ partnerships	alliances/ partnerships
					ecology/ society

increased dynamic complexity

formal organizational activity-structure that distributes roles according to a rigorous plan, rather than by the insight and preference of company chieftains. At this stage, the classical "scientific management" concepts of Frederick Taylor are applied without drawbacks, since the enterprise needs structure and organization above all. However, sooner or later, the dynamic of organizational evolution overtakes this stage as well. Managers find that if they are to sustain the competitivity of the enterprise, they must shift into a new organizational mode.

The third, or systemic, stage in the evolution of the enterprise modifies the focus of activity and attention of managers. They become less structure- and task-centered, more process- and outward-looking. They develop a fresh concern with "soft" factors, such as corporate culture, identity, and philosophy. The mature organization becomes an ongoingly self-organizing open system, capable of learning through interaction among collaborators and divisions, and between them and the larger (and no longer strictly "outside") world of suppliers, distributors, clients, and customers.

In the systemic stage, top management ceases to create blueprints and command-structures and concentrates instead on the equally demanding but no longer hierarchical tasks of facilitation and empowerment. The enterprise evolves into a self-organizing interface between its profit-generating production or service processes, and the economic, social, and ecologic setting into which these processes enter and with which they interact.

The hallmark of the systemic stage is openness to energy and information flows. The information to which the organization responds includes not only professional reports, such as marketing data, resource availability, financial performance, and technological developments, but information relative to processes in industry, society, and nature. Key elements of the enlarged information base are current and prospective state regulations, the evolution of values and preferences in the public, and cross-impacts with processes in nature.

As Figure 3.1 also shows, when these stages of enterprise evolution unfold, the firm grows additional dimensions. The first and most basic dimension is the human and physical infrastructure. This means people working with tools, much as they have done since the dawn of civilization. But the tools they work with in today's enterprises include computers, telephones, data-banks, slide rules, and computerized robots; and the people who work with these tools are not only factory workers, but technicians and engineers, team leaders, and middle and top managers.

People working with tools within an organized setting make up the enterprise's *infrastructural dimension*. In any but the smallest and simplest firm (and then only in its initial stage), this basic dimension is insufficient: it is soon joined by others. People need to eat and maintain themselves and their family—they must earn wages. Tools need to be acquired, maintained, and replaced. This calls for funds, which in turn require financial management. Also, roles and tasks need to be distributed and relations between them established. The organization must provide both for the division of tasks and responsibilities, and for their integration within a functioning whole. Consequently, a further dimension of the enterprise grows over the first—the *structural dimension*.

Structure orients function: the higher second dimension regulates and organizes the first, more basic dimension. Structure, however, is not the mechanical concept that Frederick Taylor took it to be. Creating an organizational structure in today's world means creating an open system with people, equipment, process technology, corporate culture, financial capital, and knowledge. Such a system has both an outward, formal and rule-bound aspect, and an inner, interpersonal one. Enterprises are systems with inherent goals and purposes. These factors need to be articulated, so they can be shared and elaborated.

We can identify the third dimension grown by the contemporary enterprise as the *cultural dimension*. (Here, of course, "culture" refers to organizational culture, and not to arts and literature.) In the initial stage this cultural dimension is almost entirely lacking, and in the developmental stage it is mainly tacit. It comes into its own only in the mature systemic stage. Here questions of corporate identity, purpose, and philosophy become urgent and imperative: they require serious attention. Defining identity, purpose, and philosophy is a collaborative task in which all people in the enterprise participate, but articulating these concepts for practical use in the running of the enterprise remains a task for management. It is an important task, for an articulate corporate culture clarifies goals and objectives, and provides the criteria for choosing between alternative strategies for pursuing the goals and reaching the objectives.

As the firm shifts from the interim developmental stage to the mature systemic stage, both its internal and its external relations become reorganized. Internal relations are restructured for distributed responsibilities, roles, and tasks; external relations are newly structured through flexible networking. These may include supplier, marketing, and consumer clubs, strategic partnerships, and civic activities. In manufacturing companies corporate attention becomes vastly expanded: it embraces the entire product cycle from conception to the final disposal of the end products.

Convergence with nature—known as ecological interdependence—has been a fundamental feature of the maturing of the enterprise. Its roots go back to the dawn of current ecological concerns in the 1960s. Rachel Carson's seminal *Silent Spring*, published in 1962, made only brief mention of the role of business corporations in environmental issues, including but an oblique reference to cases of cancer, lung disease, and liver poisoning among industrial workers.[1] Environmental problems were government-inflicted, and they were to be government-remedied. Since the 1980s, however, the industrial enterprise became seen as the principal agent responsible for pollution and for ecological disasters. With the exception of the nuclear meltdown at Chernobyl, most ecological disasters were ascribed to the acts of private corporations. They include Union Carbide's pesticide plant explosion in Bhopal, India; the Exxon *Valdez* oil spill off the coast of Alaska; and the Sandoz spill of toxic chemicals into the Rhine. Links have appeared between the ozone hole in the atmosphere and CFCs manufactured by chemical giants; between deforestation in Brazil and the activities of mining and lumber companies; between global warming and sulfur, carbon monoxide, and carbon dioxide pollution by smokestack industries; and between the accumulation of solid industrial wastes (such as slags, acids, ashes, and other industrial byproducts) and the poisoning of agricultural land and community water supplies.

In the mature systemic stage, managers realize that corporate profits depend heavily on their products being "environmentally friendly," that is, nontoxic, biodegradable, recycled, or recyclable. A growing segment of customers is willing to pay a premium for such products, selecting them over less adapted rival brands. Leading corporations appoint directors for environmental affairs, in many cases as part of the top management team. Since 1990, 100 percent of Dutch transnational companies and the majority of German and Japanese companies has a board member entrusted with environmental responsibilities. In many industries, CEOs devote as much as a third of their time to ecological issues. The three leading U.S. tuna canners decided that their fish must be caught by "dolphin-friendly" methods; Marks and Spencer, a British retail chain, made sure that the beef it sold did not graze on deforested Brazilian pastures; and Loblaws, a Canadian grocery retailer, decided to place only "green" products on its shelves. At the same time, leading managers realize that if their company is to appear environmentally friendly, they must not only sell "friendly" products, but also must ensure that the products are manufactured in ecologically adapted ways, and are used, and ultimately disposed, by customers in "friendly" ways. Some European companies pioneered ecology-minded sales and marketing programs. Some—Ricard, Guigoz, Chocolat Cote d'Or—contributed to ecological causes proportionately to their sales; others—among them, Swiss pharmaceutical Sandoz—created special foundations dedicated in part to remedying the environmental damage they have incurred.

Whether for genuine concern for ecological sustainability or in expectation of increased sales, higher stock valuation, and less government regulation, managers in mature enterprises have come to accept ecological responsibilities as part of their managerial tasks. And for younger executives coming from environmentally conscious management training schools, ecological and social responsibilities are integral parts of business sense.

Intensifying ties with its larger industrial, social, political, and ecological environment drives the contemporary enterprise toward the mature evolutionary stage. The mature, third-stage enterprise converges with other enterprises; with business, social, and political communities; as well as with regenerative processes in nature. Its evolving activities form hypercycles that coordinate its energy-, information-, and raw material–processing activities with ecological cycles in nature, as well as with the activities and needs of its suppliers, distributors, clients, and consumers. Increasingly, the range of its cooperation embraces partners within industry clusters, competitors within market sectors, and civic and public organizations in the states and communities where it operates. Today's market leaders create entire "business ecologies," interlinking cooperating firms in mutual-interest partnerships—the key elements underlying the success of companies such as Wal-Mart, Intel, and Microsoft.

The stage-to-stage evolution of the enterprise is constant, but it is not smooth and linear. From time to time, companies evolve critical instabilities: points of bifurcation in their progressive evolution. At these points, managers must take crucial decisions. The decisions they take determine how, and even whether, their enterprise evolves. Wrong decisions strand it at its already achieved stage; right decisions enable it to leap from one stage to the next.

The evolution of the individual enterprise repeats the evolutionary path traced by the evolution of typical enterprises in the course of history. In the early phases of the first industrial revolution, most enterprises were run like medieval shops and workshops: informally, on the initiative and at the discretion of their founders. With the coming of age of the industrial revolution in England and Germany, the informal structure of the previous epochs no longer sufficed: growing enterprises began to make use of sophisticated technologies and switched from handcrafted processes to mass production. The heyday of this stage in the historical evolution of enterprises was reached in the first half of the twentieth century, when Taylor's scientific management strategies together with Ford's assembly-line rationalization of production led to the creation of giant manufacturing companies. When rapid developments in technologies as well as markets called for more flexibility than the Taylor-Ford system could provide, the kind of hierarchic matrix organization typified by Alfred Sloane's General Motors began to change in turn into the contemporary systemic mold. The last twenty years witnessed an accelerating trend toward restructuring the rigidly hierarchic developmental-stage enterprise into the flexibly network-like systemic organization typical of Wal-Mart, Intel, and Microsoft, as well as of Time-Warner, ABB, ATT, and other national and global players.

RE-ENVISIONING THE ENTERPRISE

The recent evolution of the enterprise calls for revising a major part of the currently operative corpus of management concepts. Present-day management practice still rests on the time-honored foundations of neoclassical economics. This has proven its usefulness in the past, but the knowledge it conveys is aging rapidly. Its sum-of-the-parts approach to the enterprise gives a static, bottom-up view that is poorly adapted to convey a true picture of the complex and dynamic interactions that hallmark the mature company, both in regard to its internal operations and its external relations.

The obsolescence of the operative assumptions of the neoclassical framework—above all, the neoclassical theory of the firm—is due mostly to the fact that within mature, third-stage companies the separability of individual activities is rapidly disappearing. Scientists are assuming roles in manufacturing, manufacturing engineers are developing skills in design, marketing personnel are learning the constraints of production, and so on. The separation of internally oriented and externally keyed activities is disappearing as well. Activities "within" the organization are closely interfaced with people "outside": with customers, suppliers, distributors, partners, even competitors.

These changes mean that executives need to re-think the concepts through which they have classically viewed the firm. Describing the organization as a set of sequentially ordered parts no longer captures its essential properties. In its place they need to use a dynamic and integrated model such as shown in Figure 3.3. It pictures the enterprise as an open system transforming the flows that enter it and leave it—flows of information, energy, and materials.

The paradigm notion for understanding the functioning of the enterprise is the open system. These are systems that have a throughput of energy, matter, and/or information. The concept, as we see in Figure 3.4, applies to the enterprise. This is a system that takes in information, energy, and raw materials, and transforms them into commercially value-added products and services. The proportion of these inputs and outputs varies with the industry branch: in heavy industries, such as steel, raw materials and energy dominate; in service-industries, such as health care and computer software, information is the dominant flow.

Figure 3.4 pictures the operations of the enterprise as the application, through its personnel, of operative information, working capital, and physical infrastructure to "do work" (in the business as well as the physics sense of the term). Work—in the physics sense—produces entropy, that is, it uses up the free energies with which it is performed. This calls for an ongoing replenishing of the free energy supply. The inflow of fresh energy constitutes the negative of the entropy produced in the system: it offsets and balances the latter. Consequently, the enterprise can continue to "do work" (in the physics sense of the term). This process is basic for all real-world systems, whether they are brain cells or business companies.

Also the input of matter into the enterprise needs to be replenished, regardless of whether this involves paper clips, computer tape, or iron ore. Last, but not least, a continuous flow of information is required. The importance of fresh information is greater in a changing environment than in a static one, since information that produced good results yesterday may not produce it today, and could become entirely counter-functional tomorrow.

How the enterprise performs work can be best understood through another theoretical concept: the cross-catalytic cycle. Cross-catalytic cycles—pictured in Figure 3.5—were discovered by Nobel laureate physicist Manfred Eigen. They have proven to be almost universal in nature—basic to life itself. The reason for this is that such cycles are highly resistant to perturbation. In changing environments, where other types of cycles and structures are fatally disrupted, systems operating by means of catalytic cycles manage to survive. Thus they have been privileged by natural selection in the trials and errors of species-forming macroevolution.

Figure 3.3
Dynamical Systems View of the Enterprise

"STATIC MODEL"

"MOVING PICTURE"

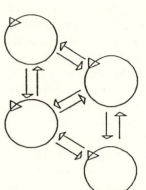

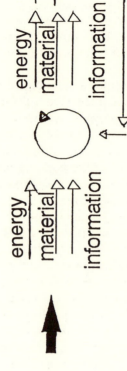

DETAILED ACTIVITY MAP

← PRODUCTS →

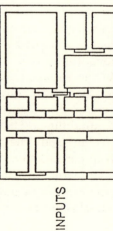

DYNAMIC ACTIVITY NETWORK

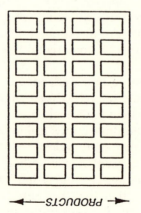

INPUTS

FLOW →

OUTPUTS

ACTIVITY LINKAGES/GROUPS

energy
material
information

energy
material
information

Figure 3.4
The Enterprise as an Open System: The Basic Flows

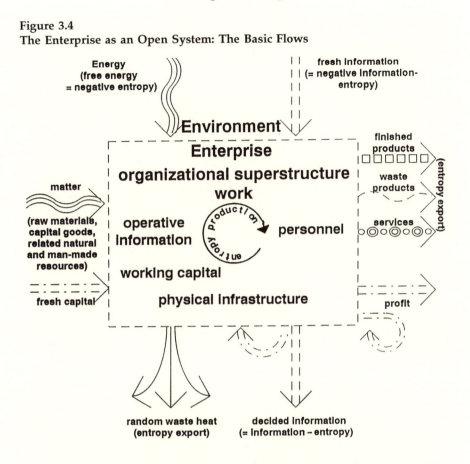

Catalytic cycles exist at all levels of organization, in nature as well as in the human world. If we take Figure 3.5 and place nucleic acids in the circles, we get the catalytic cycle that forms the basis of the living cell. If we take a cycle consisting of living cells themselves, we obtain the basic mechanism of a functionally integrated multicellular organism. And if we picture a catalytic cycle with human beings, we get a functionally integrated multiperson organism: an organization, a community or a political system.

When humans form catalytic cycles, there are many possibilities for creating functional organizations. The possibilities include organizations with technological components: here the whole cycle is committed to some form of production or service. Such an organization is the business enterprise, whether in the public or in the private sector.

Cross-catalytic cycles are evident both within corporations and between the corporation and its environment. Within corporations, product development groups receive information from sales teams and financial

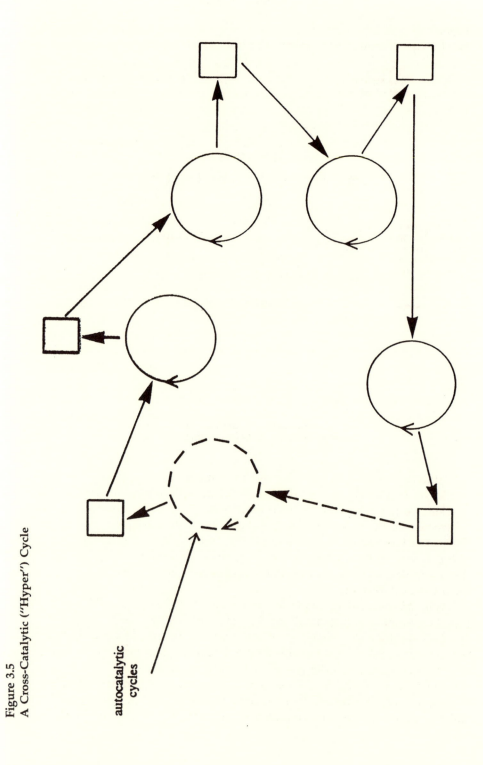

Figure 3.5
A Cross-Catalytic ("Hyper") Cycle

autocatalytic
cycles

managers and send out information about their work progress. The same is true for manufacturing teams, purchasing departments, business development managers, and so on: each "team" creates by its activity the conditions in which other teams can perform their functions, one team acting as a catalyst for the functions of the other. Without the existence of cross-catalytic cycles within a firm, the processes of learning and of adaptation to change would be difficult and slow.

The evolutionary path followed by cross-catalytic cycles leads to convergence. Each cycle feeds on itself, develops itself, and converges toward a cycle on the next higher level of organization. Thus loosely connected departments become integrated parts of divisions; divisions become subsystems of the corporation; the corporation becomes increasingly bound up in the activities of the industry; and the activities of the industry become inextricably linked to cycles occurring in the public and ecologic sectors.

Between the corporation and its business environment arises an interactive system with both auto- and cross-catalytic cycles (see Figure 3.6). One firm acts as a catalyst for other firms, both vertically through suppliers and distributors, horizontally through competitors, and increasingly what we can think of as "diagonally" through firms in related industries and through them to ecologies and to society. The entire, system forms a "business ecology" with quasi-organic properties; any one player within the ecology is dependent on the welfare of all or most of the others for profitability and growth.

Cross-catalytic cycles also exist between business ecologies and the larger ecology consisting of economic, social, and ecological components. The result is a multilevel system built like a Russian doll: with cycles within cycles within cycles. The logic of this encompassing system is the logic of fractals: it is the self-same repetition of a given pattern on successively larger (or smaller) dimensions.

While the logic of the emerging business world is that of fractals, its change-dynamics is that of the EGT. Each cycle feeds on itself, develops itself, and converges toward a cycle on the next higher organizational level. The sequence of catalytic cycles arises from the physical basis of life all the way to the evolving business ecology spanning the globe. And that ecology itself rises toward the worldwide economic and social system in which it operates.

THE EDGE OF INSIGHT

The changing realities of the enterprise require managers to complement the classical piecemeal approach to management with an evolutionary systems approach. The benefits of the evolutionary approach

Figure 3.6
**The Two Kinds of Catalytic Cycles that Interlock Enterprises and
Environments**

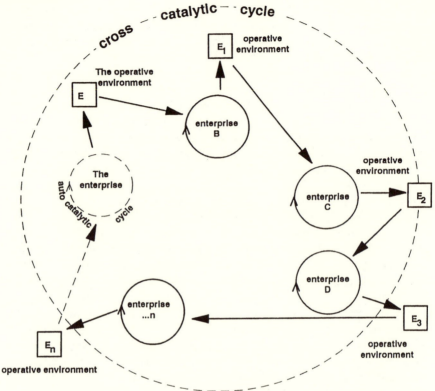

In the context of the catalytic cycles that interlock enterprises and environments, each
enterprise masters the autocatalytic cycle by which it renews its resources, its infrastructure,
and even its personnel. Each enterprise, however, obtains the resources for its operations
and self-reproduction from its environment; and the environment is also the recipient of
its products and services, as well as its wastes. What one enterprise does to its environment
affects therefore the other enterprises. The way enterprises process themselves and their
environment adds up to the cross-catalytic cycle of the entire business ecology. This affects
all enterprises and all environments and feeds ultimately back to each. In consequence a
well-managed enterprise operates by pragmatic altruism: it evolves its environment,
helping to evolve all enterprises sharing it, and by that token it evolves itself.

match those that managers expect to derive from the classical techniques:
lower costs, higher value-added, and increased shareholder returns. But
such benefits cannot be sourced uniquely in separate activities. The focus
must be on linkages between activities and functions, on information
flows, and on positioning oneself within a rapidly changing industry
sector and its social and natural milieu. These are the practical matters

to which we turn next, as we outline the action-principles that flow from the latest scientific insights on complex system evolution and the unfolding global trends.

NOTE

1. Rachel Carson, *Silent Spring* (New York: Houghton Mifflin, 1962), p. 194.

Part II

An Insightful Basis for Action

Knowledge is the new capital.

—Peter F. Drucker

Chapter 4

Eighteen Principles of Evolutionary Management

The principles of evolutionary management are not simple recipes, not even recipes for what used to be called elements of competitive advantage. Strategic focus, operational efficiency, and an effective shared company culture continue to be necessary factors in the equations that determine corporate success, yet increasingly they are not the sole factors. The classical recipes of growth and profitability need to be complemented by further principles in the management of rapidly evolving companies.

Principles such as those outlined here are basic, but they are not yet adequately understood and applied. Although not as easily quantified as traditional tools and approaches, evolutionary systems principles offer powerful insights into the mosaic of operational details which confront managers; they integrate the mosaic's properties and specify its dynamics. It is only through a clearly integrated systemic view with a specified dynamics that executives can act effectively in the changing corporate environment.

In this chapter we state, specify, and illustrate three varieties of evolutionary management principles: principles relating to the organization of the enterprise, long-term strategy-related principles, and day-to-day operational principles (see Figure 4.1).

Figure 4.1
The Key Principles of Evolutionary Management

The Organizational Principles

Org/1   Re-Cast Leaders as Stewards and Teachers

Org/2   Support Interaction and Consensus among Teams at All Levels of the Enterprise

Org/3   Create Parallel Processing Capabilities in the Organization

Org/4   Replace Hierarchies with Multilevel Heterarchies

Org/5   "Organicize" the Work Environment

Org/6   Instill Enough Permanent Instability in the Organization to Create Adaptive, Learning-Based Work Environments

Org/7   When Radical Change Is Needed, Engender Transient Chaos

Org/8   Globalize the Company Culture by "Internationalizing" Coordinating Functions and "Localizing" Operating Functions

The Strategic Principles

S/1   In Maximizing Shareholder Value, Place the People of the Company before All Other Financial, Economic, and Technological Resources and Objectives

S/2   Continually Monitor and Adjust Strategic Positioning within the Industry System

S/3   Maintain a Consistent Long-Term Competitive Focus

S/4   Treat Information as a Strategic Resource, Not as an Overhead

S/5   Compete for Sustainable Industry-Level Advantage

The Operational Principles

Op/1   Anticipate Quality through Evolutionary Dynamics and Open-System Marketing

Op/2   Include Variety Costs and the Cost of Linkages between Activities

Op/3   Compute Ecological Constraints and Opportunities and Internalize Their Cost

Op/4   Use Instability and Discontinuous Change for Competitive Advantage

Op/5   Forecast to Multiple Horizons by Extrapolating the Future, Not the Past

THE ORGANIZATIONAL PRINCIPLES

Org/1: Re-Cast Leaders as Stewards and Teachers

Precis: The trend toward decentralization and diffusion of decision-making processes is fundamentally changing the role of top management by increasing the need for, and the importance of, capable and autonomous operating personnel. This in turn is changing the role of top management, from boss and commander to coordinator and facilitator.

Traditionally leaders were seen as special people who set direction, make key decisions, and energize the troops. They were viewed as emerging from a Darwinian process of natural selection, becoming "top dog" or "captain of industry" because of superior managerial capabilities—or at least fighting abilities. Once installed in their high office, their authority was used primarily to make "big maneuvers" concerning corporate-level resources. It also extended through the ranks in the form of oral and written directives. In an evolutionary management setting, however, leadership has a different role: to give direction to the future of the enterprise through plans, scenarios, options, and strategic goals; and to create conditions for self-learning throughout the organization.

In their book *Managing for Excellence*, Bradford and Cohen analyze the management styles that are effective in a complex and rapidly changing environment.[1] They describe the style of the classical top manager as the "heroic" leader and argue that it is not efficient in organizations where the tasks entailed by executive decisions are complex, specialized, and subject to change. Heroic leaders function well in stable environments; or in enterprises where the subsidiary tasks are well-defined; or where interactions among subordinates are limited; or in organizations where the degree of control is rigorously defined. Heroic leadership can also function well where the chief possesses far more knowledge than the subordinates, and remains informed day by day. All these cases, however, are typical of enterprises of a bygone era. In today's mature enterprises, change is the only constant, and no individual, no matter how clever and well-positioned, can possess, and keep up with, all the information required to make wise decisions.

Although a heroic management style can be highly motivating for the top manager, it is precisely the contrary for everyone else. It robs people of a sense of responsibility, and the assurance that their views and insights count in the decision-making process.

In mature companies, the role of leadership involves far more subtle but no less important tasks. In such companies, the fundamental role of management is to enable the employees to achieve harmonized job performance through shared goals and values. Management's key tasks, according to Peter Drucker, are:

- to make people capable of joint performance by building on their strengths;
- to develop, set, and exemplify common goals, shared values, and simple, clear, and unifying objectives to which everyone can be committed;
- to ensure continued growth for the organization and for each individual through training and personal development;
- to build a foundation through communication and the responsibility of each person;

- to emphasize, measure, and continually improve company performance with attention to the development of the human capital; and
- to base results on what happens outside the company—a satisfied customer, a healed patient, or an individual who is learning and knows how to apply his or her learning.[2]

In a mature company, managers are designers, stewards, and teachers, responsible for building organizations where people expand their capabilities for understanding complexity. They define the challenges and visions of the future, and make decisions and execute actions that are relevant to the enterprise as a whole.

Indeed, the chief executive officers of leading companies tend to give nonconventional descriptions of their role: traffic policeman, orchestra conductor, interpreter, critic, or cheerleader. They seldom (if ever) view themselves as chief or boss.

Org/2: Support Interaction and Consensus among Teams at All Levels of the Enterprise

Precis: In an optimally organized enterprise, each member of a team thinks and feels what the others think and intend. This kind of consensus provides enormous synergistic effects within operations. The key to creating it is for management to create optimal conditions, and provide unhesitating support, for teamwork at all organizational levels.

Consultant Charles Keefer once described how in a large corporation the members of a product development team became committed to a shared vision of a dramatic new product, which the team managed to bring to market in one-third the normal time. Once the vision of the product and how they would develop it began to crystallize, Keefer noted, the team began to work in an extraordinary way. The whole became greater than the sum of the parts; that is, the progress of the whole team was greater than the sum of the progress each individual team member could have achieved alone.

In many ways, the capacity of an enterprise to operate with optimal productivity requires an open, information-efficient approach that empowers people to think for themselves, with leaders able to provide full support, active coordination, and effective facilitation. In small, highly interactive teams, employees can communicate with each other easily, and have greater pride in their work—and managers can collaborate closely, making themselves available whenever strategic decisions have to be made. In the right conditions, an enterprise can achieve gains in operational efficiency through learning processes that turn rapidly into a new competitive edge. This lesson has been learned by companies such as EDS, Intel, and Microsoft, where people work on projects in teams, rather than perform routine jobs in accordance with rigid job descriptions. It has also been learned by manufacturing companies, beginning with the Japanese firms Toyota, Yamaha, and Hitachi, where an average of 30, and never more than 300, workers are allowed in a production unit, and subplants have their own engineering and maintenance functions and materials management. In other companies, the responsibilities of mixed teams are allowed to change over time, as the members move from project to project, often working on, or sharing in, several at the same time. They work under one or more project leaders but, as Tom Peters found, essentially they "report to each other."

In a team-based organization, the function of management is to create the conditions under which project teams can operate. Managers provide the information that enables the team members to make the necessary operative decisions; they do not consider them to be employees filling preconceived niches beyond which they have neither interests nor responsibilities. In such an organization, the conventional job, as William Bridge's 1994 cover story "The End of the Job" in *Fortune* magazine predicted, has already come to an end.

Org/3: Create Parallel Processing Capabilities in the Organization

Precis: Wherever possible, greater decision-making power must be shifted to field personnel, who need to be empowered to think, act, and learn in the light of local conditions, although always in clear view of the enterprise's overall needs and objectives.

Specialists in artifical intelligence used to think that the most efficient robots would be those with a single centralized "learning-deciding" capability to confront all eventualities. This expectation proved illusory. No robot could be built that could meet the exigencies even of a reasonably complex environment; the combinatorial space of possibilities soon surpassed the computing power of the most sophisticated central processor. However, it turned out that, in order to function successfully, it is enough to connect distinct local information-processing centers with each other and subject them to a simple algorithm (for example, the instruction that at least three of the many legs of the self-navigating robot must be on the ground at any one time). Such a "decentralized learning robot" managed to navigate a far more complex terrain than any centralized-decider robot could.

The fact is that complex multicomponent systems, whether human or artificial, rarely function well on a centralized basis. In order to deal with the specifics of local activities, an empowered field organization is required, that is, able to learn and act in light of local conditions but in accordance with global corporate objectives.

Just how decentralization is to be implemented depends on the conditions necessary for self-learning—conditions that are determined mainly by the flow of the information on the basis of which relevant decisions are made. In some cases, multidisciplinary task forces need to be created with limited duration; in others, otherwise isolated individuals and functions need to be interfaced; and in still others, information-flows between top management and front-line personnel need to be facilitated and structured through iterative learning processes.

However, certain activities, such as purchasing and R&D, provide significant economies of scale or of experience; and to realize these economies, a higher degree of centralization is required. Even without the benefits of economies of scale and of experience, in some cases functions such as pricing and credit policies are best handled on a centralized basis. Yet the centralization of such operations must always be tempered with functional decentralization in others. The applicable model is not the human organism—a centralized entity governed by the brain and higher nervous system—but the decentralized learning robot.

Org/4: Replace Hierarchies with Multilevel Heterarchies

Precis: Corporations with markets and materials-flows on a global scale require organizational structures that enable them to access, process, and flexibly and efficiently act on information. This calls for functionally decentralized multilevel organizations. Such organizations are not hierarchic but heterarchic: that is, they allow significant autonomy vertically and significant coordination horizontally, permitting information and task allocation to flow "diagonally" across the various divisions and levels.

As noted in Chapter 4, when corporations reach a critical size and complexity, informal structures, based on personal charisma or competence, no longer work. At that point, viable firms shift to a more organized matrix structure. However, as multiple interfaces increase both within the enterprise and between the enterprise and its relevant environment, the matrix structure begins to prove inadequate. The majority of globally operating companies learned this lesson—as did ABB some years ago and Lafarge, ATT, and General Motors more recently—they transformed from top-heavy matrix organizations into flexibly coordinated network-like structures.

Multiple levels of decision-making bring multiple advantages. Catalytic cycles bind the various levels, coordinating the function of units, departments, and divisions so as to ensure that each part contributes optimally to the purposes of the whole. The cycles optimize the use of limited resources by integrating allocations in view of system-wide needs. Moreover, multiple levels create the flexibility to engender localized change, without involving other than the relevant parts of the enterprise in the change process.

Multilevel organizations are in a better position to respond effectively and creatively to the demands of a changing business environment than classical hierarchic organizations. A heterarchic organization can come up with strategies that are more adequate to the demands of the times than the best thought-out strategy excogitated at headquarters and enforced by vertically extended hierarchic structures.

Managing a heterarchic system does not call for rigid control at the highest level, but for downward delegation and interlevel coordination. The so-called "subsidiarity principle" can apply: decisions are to be made at the lowest level where they are effective. There must be rules, however, for cycling to higher levels; for example, to consult a higher echelon before incurring capital expenditures beyond a certain amount. By this method top management is spared the all-too-frequent temptation to get involved in "choosing the color of the furniture" at each level of the organization.

In heterarchies, top management is not required to specify goals and the means of achieving them at each level, but can set an overall course for operations one level down. Even more important, it can create the conditions at the subsidiary levels for learning and making decisions of their own. Thereby an open cascade of delegated decision-making can result, combining the flexibility of goal-conscious coordination with the efficiency of drawing on field insight and experience.

Org/5: "Organicize" the Work Environment

Precis: The new information, communication, and related technologies create physical and mental burdens on a company's collaborators that are analogous to the primary physical burdens placed on industrial workers in the last century. The evolutionary management approach shapes the work environment for physical and functional adaptation to the current needs of the enterprise's information-loaded collaborators.

In this century scientific management practices, with their optimized work flow and attempted elimination of non-productive activities, have taken their toll on the ranks of corporate staff. Efforts to convert from a paper-based to a computer-based office, and to convert from a semi-automatic to a fully automatized factory floor, have led to alienation, stress, fatigue, frustration, and on occasion even to mental and physical illness. In the contemporary enterprise such conditions must be urgently rectified.

A key principle of evolutionary management is the creation of an "organicized" environment for productive work. Such an environment is both physically and functionally suited to the bodily and mental well-being of people. The organicized office allows and even encourages spontaneous human interaction in the course of productive work. Access to collaborators is facilitated, both in the workplace and in shared eating and recreational facilities. The organicized work environment does not do away with face-to-face communication. Personal contact is needed for efficient teamwork and for creating and reinforcing learning processes—accomplishments that cannot be achieved over faceless networks, no matter how well they may be structured and efficiently operated. But personal contact is always voluntary. The walls of individual work spaces are insulated and soundproofed; lighting is clear but not harsh; colors are harmonious; the furnishings are esthetic as well as functional. Natural and recyclable materials are used rather than nonbiodegradable synthetics. The difficult bodily requirements of working with computers and related information and communication hardware are compensated through ergonomic seats and desks to eliminate or reduce fatigue, neck and backaches, and stiffness in arms and hands.

The wide range of information and communication techniques and technologies currently in use are integrated within a company-wide information and communication system. Software, hardware, networks, desk-to-desk link-ups and their peripherals, workstations, control rooms, and heavy equipment are part of an integrated system that includes the value-added step, data-processing, as well as communication.

Organicizing the workplace permits greater flexibility in the choice of the physical location for performing work. Certain tasks, such as research and development, programming, marketing, design, budgeting, planning, and project evaluation, can take place wherever the individual who is responsible for them prefers. This may be the company workplace, the home, the company car, or a hotel room on business trips. Many jobs allow a flexible mix of locations, suited to the preferred lifestyle of individuals.

Org/6: Instill Enough Permanent Instability in the Organization to Create Adaptive, Learning-Based Work Environments

Precis: In periods of rapid and turbulent change in the external competitive environment, internal organizational cultures that emphasize stability can produce complacency. Conversely, organizational cultures that succeed in institutionalizing instability can be factors of adaptation and learning for middle and upper managers. Institutionalized instability can work, however, only if it does not become excessive, and only if it is balanced by measurable objectives and counterbalancing benefits.

Western business managers have long been taught that their performance is measured according to two basic parameters: the achievement of quantifiable goals, and the ability to maintain stability in their organizations and work relationships. The rise of large multinational corporations, and their personnel policy of rotating managers across operating units, has accentuated this need to produce specifiable results in a short period of time within an organization that has a defined identity and culture.

Although much has been written about the shortcomings of quarterly goal-oriented management styles compared with a Japanese style that is long-term and process-oriented, little has been said directly about the constant drive for stability. The need to resolve corporate tensions, the emphasis on harmonious working relationships, the search for new levels of financial performance, the drive to limit personnel turnover, are the natural outcome of a goal-oriented management style. Periods of transformation and turbulence are accepted only as a means to achieve better ends.

Notions of "turbulence" and "chaos" in corporate culture are gaining fashion through the writings of management gurus such as Tom Peters and Charles Handy, yet they are phenomena that the majority of managers avoid. Periods of instability are accepted only if they are precisely that—periods. Yet businesses must go through phases that "shake up" an organization that has grown uncompetitive, or radically rethink approaches to customer service, or else question the company's core business positioning.

Few managers today believe that for themselves and their organizations instability should be a permanent way of life. Few espouse that "living on the edge" with a sustained psychological discomfort will lead to better performance for them and their businesses. Yet it is becoming increasingly apparent that in large and complex corporations, the ongoing existence of instability in the layers of middle and upper managers is increasingly a success factor. Conversely, management styles which attempt to control complex organizations with a gradualist approach, or which attempt to force them into stable states during phases of inherent instability, are proving to be far less performable than styles that usher in discontinuous change and use chaos to shift to new and more competitive levels.

"The bad news is that it is very tiring," said the vice-chairman of Lafarge, remarking about the stress that his managers bear from permanent instability, "the good news is that it is very motivating." The challenge for the company's leaders is to create enough discomfort for learning and productivity to be optimized. Too much stress leads to demotivation, neglect of work, and ultimately paralysis.

The approach to productive instability is necessarily an overall package. A constant re-setting of performance objectives, combined with tight financial controls on resources, can only work if a well-understood vision and a high level of salary and benefits are linked to results. Managers who are forced to make autonomous decisions (i.e., without much corporate or external support) in uncertain and rapidly changing environments will only be effective if the measures of success are clear. Restructuring an organization requires a transparent and impartial vision of the target structure of the organization, and of the process by which to achieve that structure.

Org/7: When Radical Change Is Needed, Engender Transient Chaos

Precis: In contrast with the traditional belief that chaos is pure disorder, evolutionary management shows that transient turbulence can revitalize outdated structures and renew obsolete procedures. It can create openness to undertake flexible adjustments leading to the more thorough and radical forms of innovation that are sometimes required to cope with emerging threats and seize fresh opportunities.

In the business enterprise, as in society at large, occasional chaos is a "normal" occurrence that need not elicit surprise and must not cause confusion. Whenever a complex system approaches a critical threshold in its evolution, it encounters transient chaos. The resulting bifurcation has irreversible consequences: the organization is unlikely to return to the conditions that characterized its prior state. The chaotic condition provides an ideal opportunity to wipe the slate clean and evolve the organization toward a more orderly and better-adapted state. To achieve new order following transient chaos, one need not try to reduce the pressure in hopes of returning to a previous state. On the contrary, as Figure 4.2 illustrates, one can often "push through" to the next level of order.

Periods of chaos also offer an excellent opportunity to streamline and

Figure 4.2
Lessons from Hydrodynamics

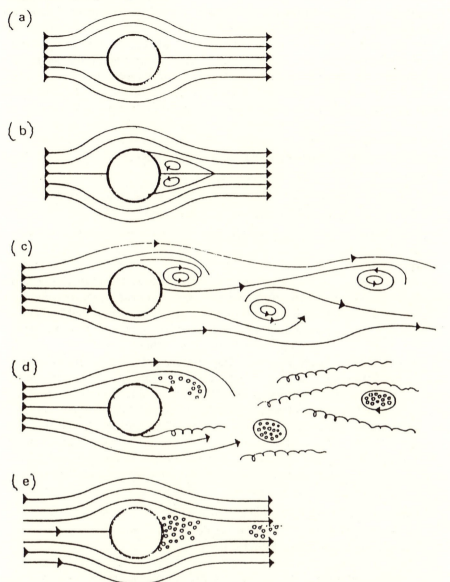

(a)

(b)

(c)

(d)

(e)

Lessons from hydrodynamics: turbulence (a form of chaos) born of intensifying pressure gives way to new order as the pressure increases beyond a critical point. Above: the relative movement of a liquid and a solid object creates and overcomes turbulence in a continuous sweep. (a) The flow pattern is smooth and orderly. (b) Preliminary perturbations appear. (c) Turbulence spreads. (d) The flow becomes entirely turbulent. (e) The flow settles into a new pattern of order. (The so-called Reynolds number [given by speed of flow times diameter of solid object divided by viscosity of the liquid] increases monotonously from (a) to (e), as laminary flow becomes turbulent and turns [partially] laminary again.) The solid object can be stationary, as a stake in a stream, or moving, as a raft in still water.

update the company metrics. Confusing reporting with "band-aid" corrections can be disastrous: they are poorly understood and tend to confuse rather than enlighten.

Rather than submit to the uncontrolled dynamics of the changes that occur involuntarily within the organization, changes need to be triggered voluntarily by engendering transient, but adequately controlled, chaos. This can be done at all levels of the enterprise, from the departmental through the divisional to the corporate. The key to this process is to:

• change key personnel;
• produce a shared vision of the objectives to be achieved;
• communicate extensively the shared vision;
• get people to consider all alternatives except remaining with the status quo;
• adopt a team approach to implementing change; and
• provide a clear set of metrics and reports on the change that is taking place.

Whereas post-chaos goals and objectives need to be clearly envisaged, *a priori* conceptions of the strategies to be implemented after the period of chaos is over are premature and can be dangerous. It is possible, for example, to fix a goal of achieving an 18 percent return on net assets, or of reaching a 40 percent market share, without fixing the particular actions and measures through which to achieve these targets.

It is imperative that during this phase the leadership communicate regularly with managers at all levels of the organization: for the most part, people tend to be uncomfortable with chaotic conditions and worried about task achievement and even job security. The leadership needs to listen to concerns and articulate the processes as they unfold at each stage. It must not do more than set the agenda, however, allowing mixed teams of production managers, distribution managers, sales managers, and directors of personnel and heads of information services to conduct the process.

Org/8: Globalize the Company Culture by "Internationalizing" Coordinating Functions and "Localizing" Operating Functions

> *Precis: Corporate culture is enriched by the talents, experiences, and perspectives of all the countries in which the corporation operates. To make the best of the corporation's global dimension, managers involved in multicountry coordination need to be internationalized, while those who interface primarily with the external environment function best when situated in the context of the local culture.*

The geographic development of the new global companies is not always matched by their culture and organization. Some American corporations tend to pursue organizational policies abroad which are American; French corporations tend to remain French. Yet the ability to create a truly global corporation—as yet limited to a handful of top global players—is key to efficient operation in the present business environment.

The extent of an enterprise's productive globalization depends, of course, on the nature of its business. Companies such as Coca Cola require a higher level of globalization than Paramount, or Hospital Corp. of America, for example, because of greater similarities in the relevant technologies and customer purchase criteria across countries. Nevertheless, the following rules apply to corporations in general.

- *Wherever the company operates, internationalize the corporate culture, that is, diversify the home-country-based charter of values and perspectives.* Successful corporations are already acting on this principle. Increasingly, Japanese companies are sending their young executives to Western training programs, or for extended periods to foreign subsidiaries for cultural acclimatization. Lafarge, now in over 35 countries, has embarked on a major effort to internalize its culture by hiring non-French nationals; using English, German, or Spanish in management meetings; and employing transnational management practices in personnel evaluation, project analysis, budget processes, etc.

- *Create a core team of international managers with leadership and coordinating functions.* Managers who interact with local teams across countries and continents can severely hamper operations if they transpose their national perspectives to their managerial tasks. To be effective they must practice, as the ABB motto claims, "the art of being local, worldwide." International coordinating functions include corporate-level finance, strategic planning, tax concerns, legal affairs, as well as the area of human resources (recruiting, training, and development). Managers in these areas have a double function: to provide expertise in their particular area, and to adapt it to the conditions and perspectives that reign in the country where they operate. Corporate leadership, as already noted, is essentially of a "coordinating" nature. In global companies it requires, more than any other function, transnationally accultured managers, working hand-in-hand with an indigenous management team that is capable of functioning effectively in the local cultural environment.

- *Recruit and develop local managers in the operating functions.* A handful of successful enterprises have already developed internationalized general managers, capable of being German in Germany, American in the United States, and Indian in India; but the limits of this kind of adaptability are quickly apparent. Managers whose primary roles are interfacing with the local environment—customers, suppliers, distributors, partners, and state governments—are more effective if they are from the local cultural milieu than if they come from the outside. Hiring nationals to manage operations in the host country also provides a more welcome local presence, and it contributes to the globalization of the corporate culture itself.

THE STRATEGIC PRINCIPLES

S/1: In Maximizing Shareholder Value, Place the People of the Company before All Other Financial, Economic, and Technological Resources and Objectives

Precis: The time-honored function of management is to establish strategic priorities for optimizing the company's resources. In the past, strategic priorities were described in terms of financial indicators and customer satisfaction, while corporate resources were assessed primarily in technological and financial terms. In an intensely competitive and rapidly evolving environment, such assessments of priorities prove inadequate; only the full application of the dedication and creativity of the people of the company can ensure lasting competitiveness. Since a motivated and creative human resource base is the best way to optimize the company's other resources, management must give conscious and unhesitating priority to people at all levels of the organization.

If collaborators are not properly motivated, if they do not properly understand what the enterprise is about and what their role is within it, and if they are not convinced of the meaningfulness of corporate goals and their personal assignments, they will not act with the degree of creativity and commitment that is necessary to ensure success in today's business environment.

"Putting people first" is a well-worn slogan, but its content needs to be updated and rejuvenated. In the past, it signified an abstractly altruistic and moralizing attitude, designed to exhibit the good will of management more than to realize expectations of tangible benefit. This must change. With growing competition among an ever smaller number of competitors, only the wisest, not the strongest, can survive. Wisdom in this instance means collective corporate ability to act creatively and flexibly as the company navigates the turbulent waters of its market segment. In these times personnel-directed altruism becomes pragmatic: it serves the most immediate survival objectives of the enterprise. Acting on it calls for instituting a system of goal-setting, performance appraisal, and compensation that is integrated into team, divisional, and corporate results—rather than linked only to personal achievement.

S/2: Continually Monitor and Adjust Strategic Positioning within the Industry System

Precis: As shifts in technology, bargaining power, legislative constraints, and other key competitive forces occur, advantage will accrue only to those companies that continually adapt their activity positioning in the context of their particular industry system.

Companies are continually adjusting their strategic positioning in view of the changing realities of their industry sector. The objective of this repositioning is to capture the highest proportion of profit margin accruing to the industry as a whole. The factors that determine industry profit allocation include bargaining power, technology control, locus of value-added, and comparative advantage. All these factors are changing on a continuing basis. Consequently, many companies are now continually redefining their activities.

For example, insurance companies subcontract data-processing (which was their traditional activity) and enter fields such as medical services provision (through health maintenance organizations) and automotive repair service (through automobile maintenance organizations). Computer manufacturers are subcontracting the majority of their parts manufacture and entering the fields of telecommunications and consumer financing. Leading cement companies, such as Lafarge Corporation and Holderbank in the United States, are entering the waste management field through waste-derived fuels, recycling byproducts from coal combustion and steel mills, and solidifying (with special cement) the waste of others.

Decisions on activity repositioning need to be made within the context of the total industry system, since right choices depend directly on the competencies of others, the number of competitors in each activity group together with their bargaining power, and the location of value-added for the customer.

S/3: Maintain a Consistent Long-Term Competitive Focus

Precis: In fast-changing environments, sustainable management requires the establishment of a long-term corporate identity—for employees, competitors, and financial analysts as well as for customers—in ways that are recognizable and profitable, through price, volume, and stock market premiums.

Although, on first sight, it may seem contradictory to the principle of continually monitoring and adjusting the company's strategic positioning (Principle S/2), the value of maintaining a consistent long-term focus is demonstrated by successful companies that have achieved both continual strategic repositioning *and* a consistent long-term strategic objective. Volvo, for example, has changed its segment focus to luxury, and developed a crucial car and truck alliance with Renault (which has remained in effect despite the failed merger talks), all the while conserving its commitment to essentially the same kind of automobile for 25 years—conservative, functional cars that verge on the stoic and ignore fashions and trendiness. In its 160 years of existence, Lafarge has shifted its long-term competitive focus only once: in the 1960s it evolved (with the consulting help of McKinsey) from an essentially French and Canadian cement manufacturer into a global construction materials company. Its commitment to world leadership has not varied since then, while its positioning within the construction materials industry has been changing continually. (The company divested its engineering business in the 1970s, its refractory products in the early 1980s, and its bathroom ceramics division in the early 1990s, while entering the building, paints, mortars, admixtures, and specialty-products segments throughout the 1980s. In the United States it has repositioned itself through its Systech subsidiary as a waste management company.)

Other company examples of commitment to long-term competitive focus include Matsushita and Toto in home products. These are companies that have exponentially expanded their product segments, geographic coverage, and downstream activities focus, keynoted by the motto "the best in home products."

In regard to the principle of conserving their long-term competitive focus, enterprises are faced with a twofold challenge: to find the underlying coherence of their long-term strategic objectives; and to communicate it. Some companies have succeeded remarkably well, for example, General Electric with its portfolio of business units developed under Jack Welch, and its message "we bring good things to life." Other companies such as Akzo, however, reached 10 billion U.S. dollars or more in sales without achieving a widely recognized corporate identity.

S/4: Treat Information as a Strategic Resource, Not as an Overhead

Precis: As complexity rises in the competitive environment, and as information technologies (IT) become pervasive, managers must assure the enterprise's information-openness and information-efficiency as sources of strategic advantage.

In his book *Shaping the Future*, Peter Keen describes the informational reality of contemporary businesses.[3] This reality is hallmarked by the facts that:

- between 25 and 80 percent of companies' cash flows is processed on-line;
- electronic data interchange is the norm in operations;
- image-technology has become an operational necessity; and
- companies are now directly linked to major suppliers and customers in electronic partnerships.

As a result, the role and value of information has assumed new proportions.

In the new business context, information flowing from diverse sources, including science and R&D, as well as from the market and from clients and competitors, must be cost-effectively accessed, using efficient monitoring systems and information-gathering capabilities. The accessed knowledge needs to be processed and applied, among other things, to customer service, operations, marketing strategies, distribution, and the measurement of ecologic and social impacts. Not surprisingly, the choice of IT platform is fast becoming a key strategic decision, shifted out of the hands of directors of information services and into those of top management.

In conventional organizational structures, the directors of information services were responsible not only for the selection of hardware and software and for system configuration, but also for the format and occasionally even for the type of data available to the users. This often entailed serious errors. Federal Express wrote off several hundred million dollars on its Zap-Mail project; a "bug" in American Airlines' yield-management has cost 15 million dollars in lost revenues. However, it is the accumulation of smaller, less spectacular mistakes that is proving to be the most insidious. When a director of information services explains to the salespeople that reporting by product and by location is not possible on the enterprise's current IT system, the result is that, when losses occur, management cannot judge whether the product or the location was the source of the problem. When computer printouts on profit and loss show excessive comparative detail (actual results compared with the results of last year, probable this year, specific budget, etc.), the field personnel end up discarding the entire report. The solution to such problems is to prohibit IT decisions from being made by IT specialists alone. Instead, mixed teams need to be created containing IT personnel, end-users, and general management.

The strategic principle of opening the corporation to information concerns not merely a choice of technology—it has immediate consequences for overall strategy, operations, and organization. By interconnecting the various components of the corporation in an integrated set of activities, information changes roles and interrelations within the enterprise. Purchasing, forecasting, production, and inventory control turn into integrated and interdependent "on-line" activities. In actual practice, competitive, technical, legal, and managerial decisions, and the consequences, should not be separated from each other; and the actual and evolving links of the corporation to its wider industry system (suppliers, competitors, distributors, customers, regulatory agencies, subcontractors, etc.) must be treated as major determinants of profitability.

S/5: Compete for Sustainable Industry-Level Advantage

Precis: In the context of global reach and systemic interdependencies, the sustainable advantage of an enterprise is inextricably bound up with the sustainable advantage of its industry. To assure the enterprise's long-term viability, it must coevolve with its industry system including suppliers, distributors, subcontractors, and direct and indirect competitors.

It is increasingly true that the long-term viability of enterprises is linked to the soundness of the industry systems in which they operate. The commercial airlines and computer hardware industries illustrate the dangers of cutthroat competition without regard for the consequences for the overall profitability of the industry. The U.S. information and communication sector, the European pharmaceutical industry, and many Japanese-dominated industries illustrate, in turn, the benefits of partnerships, alliances, codes of behavior, and the establishment of norms and standards for all participants.

The purpose of strategic "coevolutionary" partnerships is not merely conventional risk-sharing, and such partnerships are not limited to intraindustry participation. They include foresighted linkages to create new and sustainable profit opportunities and may embrace local communities and other industries, as well as public institutions. The enterprise's future is increasingly bound up with the future of its wider social and ecologic environment, and it is only through shared responsibilities and pooled resources that it can sustain profitable development.

Strategic coevolutionary partnerships are already a reality in many spheres of business activity, and they are developing at an increasing pace. Interfirm "hypercycles" within an industry create "business ecologies" that offer conditions for the reciprocal intensification of corporate growth. (Michael Porter described this process as the "diamond" of industry clustering—the diamond being a system made up of the strategy, structure, and rivalry of firms, on the one hand, and of factor conditions, demand conditions, and related and supporting industries, on the other.[4]) This lends participating industries a crucial competitive advantage.

Unlike the mergers and acquisitions typical of the 1980s, coevolutionary partnerships enhance competitiveness rather than increase competition. Partnerships of this kind are an integral element of the functionality of business. As Japanese management consultant Kenichi Ohmae pointed out, the advent of complexity—economically, technologically, as well as culturally—requires businesses to pool their resources and cooperate, even in order to be more effective in competition.[5] Cooperation is doubly indicated if ongoing competitiveness calls for adjustments that serve not only the short-term interests of one or another company, but the enduring interests of the entire sector in which those companies operate.

Business ecologies built of hypercycles between enterprises and their social and natural milieu yield increasing benefits in the form of more qualified human resources, a nondegraded physical and living environment, and the improved long-term management of raw material stocks and other natural resources. They also avert punitive government regulations and antagonistic community activism. The coevolutionary strategy is clear: either the whole system evolves sustainably, or each actor within it risks additional costs, and may even find itself driven on the shoals.

THE OPERATIONAL PRINCIPLES

Op/1: Anticipate Quality through Evolutionary Dynamics and Open-System Marketing

Precis: When competing on quality in industries where needs and expectations are in rapid evolution, successful competitors must not only meet demand, but must also anticipate and shape it. To do so, managers must operate on the basis of a sound knowledge of the evolutionary trends that underlie changing tastes and values, creating demand for specific products and services through an open-system approach to marketing.

In today's unstable business environment, the quality circle concept of Japanese management (itself an important innovation) needs to be complemented with the evolutionary principle of anticipating and shaping demand. Quality circle concepts are implicitly feedback processes based on the present. In operations which are subject to discontinuous changes in technology or consumer expectation, these concepts do not suffice: anticipation and forward-creation of quality are required.

Forward-based thinking needs to be informed by the dynamics that govern the evolution of complex systems. Consequently, managers must not only listen carefully to what the consumer is saying today, but must also take a hand in forming what the customer will want tomorrow—based on foreseeable changes in values, technologies, tastes, and competitor offerings.

The level of sophistication and range of alternatives in today's product and service technologies are so high that consumers can no longer envisage for themselves their own "best choice." In electronic entertainment, for example, toy companies are increasingly determining for the consumer how the next generation of products will be shaped, because direct questioning of consumers, based on their present knowledge, is no longer sufficient to plan next year's product line.

For anticipatory quality to work, the currently dominant closed-system view of marketing must be replaced. Conventional marketing consists of analyzing, organizing, planning, and controlling the customer as someone who is outside the essentially closed system of the enterprise. In open-system marketing, on the other hand, the customer is an organic extension of the corporation, linked through continuous interaction with it. The new approach to marketing calls for flexible, empathic, and lateral thinking, overcoming the hard, vertical, "objective" approaches typical of the classical techniques.

Op/2: Include Variety Costs and the Cost of Linkages between Activities

Precis: Complexity in operations creates its own costs. These must be accurately reflected in analytic accounting, including feedback loops, bottlenecks, equipment set-up time, and other "variety" costs frequently incurred in multiactivity and multicountry operations.

In spite of increases in productivity at each individual value-added step, enterprises can experience increases in total cost that are not linked to factor prices. These cost-increases are often unexplained until the linkages between value-added steps are more closely examined. For example, at Allia, Lafarge's former bathroom ceramics subsidiary, fashion trends and multicountry market share increase had exponentially multiplied the number of products, shapes, and styles. The manufacturing plants that attempted to produce a large number of different shapes and styles at the same location incurred unexplained increases in unit costs, until variety costs were explicitly identified. For example, one of the value-added steps consisted of "glazing" the precast product before it went to the kiln for firing. When large, multiform, colored products were intermixed with simple, monoform, white products, the glazer had to switch over the equipment, change the pigment source, and mentally change the standards of his work (as color products are more difficult to finish). These "changeover" costs were principally reflected in *time*, rather than in direct labor (or materials) cost per product.

Minimizing time-related costs of complexity can be achieved in part through simplification. In Allia's case, the solution was to group products into homogeneous sets, shapes, and styles and allocate them to different manufacturing plants. Simple, low-end products were manufactured in Portugal, while complex, high-end products remained in France and Germany.

Feedback loops, changeover costs, information quality, and communication between activities should also be carefully monitored and controlled. Poor forecasting, combined with time-lags and data distortion through intermediate manipulation, can lead to important inventory costs as production fails to match demand. In such cases, the costs of complexity cut decisively into profits.

Op/3: Compute Ecological Constraints and Opportunities and Internalize Their Cost

> *Precis: In pursuit of sustainable growth, enterprises have a clear choice: either internalize the costs and constraints of the natural environment, or wait until government is forced to regulate operations and the public mobilizes against unwelcome practices. Making the proper choice means a calculation of profitability that is system-wide and includes the costs incurred on the company's ecologic and social interfaces.*

As today's relevant business environment embraces the ecologic and social milieu, the costs incurred in this wider setting must be assessed as internal to the company's operations rather than as external. The use of nonrenewable resources, the recycling of renewable resources, waste management, and airborne, soil, and water pollution are cost factors that belong in the corporate profit equation.

Internalizing ecologic costs calls for strategic cash flow projections that incorporate sources of revenue coming from price premiums associated with "green labels," as well as the costs of ecologic regulations and penalties. Some financial analysts shy away from the inclusion of such "green" factors partly because they are hard to quantify, and partly because they consider them somebody else's problem. However, in today's social climate, such habits are changing; only the most short-term-oriented companies persist in the traditional practices.

Both the stick and the carrot argue for a socio-ecologic system of cost accounting. Businesses need to avoid governmental regulation, which will come sooner or later if self-regulation fails. At the same time, they must avoid bad image discounts on share capital, a new equity risk affecting companies perceived as part of the "smokestack complex." Also to be averted is the corresponding danger that the competition gets the public's approbation as the industry's good player. In turn, the carrot argues that the so-called green stocks phenomenon is bound to affect stock markets worldwide, bringing premium value to equity perceived to be stewarding the environment. Computing the cost-factors in the ecologic and social milieu also promises a more intangible benefit: the value of goodwill. Good neighbors make good local partners, which is an important consideration in the turbulent social climate of today's global companies.

Op/4: Use Instability and Discontinuous Change for Competitive Advantage

Precis: Consistently with nonlinear and probabilistic change in complex systems, enterprises pass through periods of intense instability and uncertainty. Managers need to learn the art of transforming uncertainty and risk into probabilistic but self-enhancing decision-making.

Periods of heightened instability and uncertainty represent strategic breakpoints for managers: decisions taken during such periods can bifurcate the enterprise into a new stable period of growth and profitability, or can lead it into intractable decline, loss of competitive advantage, or bankruptcy. Such breakpoints are dynamic windows of opportunity for informed managers, rather than the threat to the status quo that businesspeople have traditionally taken them to be.

Most managers recognize the signs of impending instability and radical change. What is more difficult is to find the right course of action to lead beyond turbulence into calmer waters. Knowledge, insight, and creativity play a critical role in decision-making involving probabilistic processes. A sound assessment of the probabilities of nonlinear change, and a willingness to "consider everything except the status quo" become necessary. These strategies can be implemented by permitting a wider degree of creative play in the organization. The key factor is often internal openness to information exchange. Senior managers must know what is going on in the minds of front-line salespeople, factory foremen, and research designers, and front-line salespeople must understand the objectives decided on by factory foremen. It is out of the interplay between the different parts and levels of the corporate system that relevant innovations crop up, like so many fluctuations that nucleate and spread throughout the system.

Chaos theory tells informed managers that small local events offer ample scope for change at the full system level. The pertinent finding is the "butterfly effect." In complex chaotic environments, even butterflies that flap their wings can create local turbulences that spread throughout the system. In enterprises, too, small-scale changes may propagate across departments, divisions, and even between different country units. Changes at the corporate level may propagate throughout an industry sector.

Within individual enterprises, local practices that prove successful in one retail store or one manufacturing plant can become rapidly integrated into the whole corporate system. When one Wal-Mart store employed "greeters" to welcome customers in what is otherwise a relatively low-end warehouse environment, it became an instant system-wide success. Within a few years, it was not only adopted at every store, but built an image and a style that has contributed significantly to Wal-Mart's success—and to the decline of K-Mart, its principal competitor. Innovations can spread also in regard to environmental concerns. Weyerhaeuser's decision to develop loblolly pines (a species of tree that grows fast and gets by on little water) promises to be a non-negligible input to efforts to conserve the world's rain forests. Even a relatively minor decision, such as that of Ben and Jerry, a U.S. ice cream maker, to market a popular flavor called "rain forest crunch" using a nut grown in Amazonia, may have contributed in a noteworthy manner to bringing the public's ecologic consciousness closer to the threshold where it can catalyze some significant form of national action. When competitors in an industry face nonlinear transformations in the development of their sector, the ability to engage in such "creative plays with chance" is a precondition of enhanced profitability and corporate image.

Op/5: Forecast to Multiple Horizons by Extrapolating the Future, Not the Past

Precis: Enterprises need to increase flexibility and reduce delay-time in responding to discontinuous change, envisaging alternative futures based on probabilistic underlying trends. In many cases, clearing the way for new approaches calls for selectively "forgetting" past strategies, even if (and sometimes precisely because) in the past they were successful.

Time compression has become a key to successful company operation. Time-based companies, such as Honda in combustion engines and Citicorp in mortgage originations, have increased both profits and market share compared to their slower competitors. The more complex and fast-changing an industry, the greater the role of time compression. This is especially true in regard to company responses to sudden and unforeseen change in the operating environment.

Forecasting to multiple horizons can reduce response-time delays by adapting the mindset of managers to sudden and radical changes. An example of the value of this strategy was the scenario planning exercise in the late 1960s by Pierre Wack and others at Royal Dutch/Shell.[6] They produced two sets of future scenarios for the oil industry, each with its own set of projected price figures. One scenario was based on conventional wisdom about stable and low oil prices, while the other projected a price crisis triggered by facts already known before 1971. The latter included the gradual depletion of U.S. oil reserves, the steady rise in Western demand for oil, and the growing strength of militant anti-West factions within OPEC. By exploring the full ramifications of this oil price shock scenario, Shell was prepared for the change. In the following years, it rose from one of the weaker of the "Seven Sisters" to second position (after Exxon).

The point of such examples is not to extol the values of prognostication, but to indicate the importance of preparing managers for dealing with discontinuous change. By considering the possibilities associated with radically different alternative futures, managers can increase flexibility and reduce delays in the company's response time.

During planning exercises, the weight of the past invariably comes to press on the methods and models currently used. Quantification, rigor, and the grounding of issues in facts remain important indicators of past and present conditions, but they cannot be exclusively relied upon when formulating alternative futures. This is true for two reasons.

First, industry leaders increasingly create their own futures in selected markets by setting rules of business practice, specification standards, signaling competitor intentions, informing the thinking of local communities, and shaping customer expectations. This "creative influence on the future" allows companies to implement some aspects of their vision of the future rather than only to adapt to conditions that have reigned in the past.

Second, the prolongation of past strategies can be a source of disadvantage. For example, William C. Durant's configuration into General Motors of the leading automobile producers of the day—Buick, Cadillac, Oldsmobile, and Oakland—and the subsequent structure created under Alfred Sloan handicapped the company more than 50 years later when, under the weight of its nineteen individual platforms and a large bureaucracy, it lost both market share and profit to emerging Japanese competitors. Ford, on the other hand, succeeded in turning around its own declining profits and shares by 1993 in an extraordinary change of strategy that demonstrated the importance of forgetting certain elements of the past. Yet even there, the arduous route that led to the adoption of the strategy was a reminder of the difficulties companies encounter in selectively forgetting past successes. The ongoing problems faced by IBM also support the point that tried and proven strategies should not be projected into the future, no matter how successful they were in the past.

In global markets, predictions of future levels of profitability based on the current configuration of company operations often fail to come true. This may be for ecologic reasons, when costs of disposal and remediation wipe out profits, or else because growth has collapsed or technology has redefined products and services. In all such cases, leading players either break through into new fields and come up with new modes of operation, or face breakdown in the context of the established pattern.

NOTES

1. D. Bradford and A. Cohen, *Managing for Excellence: The Guide to Developing High Performance in Contemporary Organizations* (New York: John Wiley, 1984), and their forthcoming *The New Leadership* (New York: John Wiley, 1997).

2. Peter F. Drucker, *The New Realities* (New York: Harper & Row, 1990).

3. Peter Keen, *Shaping the Future: Business Design Through Information Technology* (Cambridge, Mass.: Harvard Business School Press, 1991).

4. Michael Porter, *Competitive Advantage: Creating and Sustaining Superior Performance* (New York: The Free Press, 1985).

5. Kenichi Ohmae, *The Mind of the Strategist: Business Planning for Competitive Advantage* (New York: Penguin Books, 1983).

6. Cf. Peter Schwartz, *The Art of the Long View: The Path to Strategic Insights for Yourself & Your Company* (New York: Doubleday & Co., 1991).

Chapter 5

Corporate Redesign: Mastering the Dynamics of Change

The payoff of management theory is management practice. The payoff of applying the principles of evolutionary management is a better informed and more reliable conduct of business. This applies to a wide range of practical tasks, from information management to strategic planning and organizational structuring (and restructuring) to the running of day-to-day operations. Indeed, a particularly fruitful area of the application of evolutionary principles is process redesign: the restructuring of the organization along more functional and competitive lines.

Before entering into detailed discussions of evolutionary process redesign, and illustrating redesign with actual case studies, we should discuss the nature of the endeavor itself. Why is evolutionary process redesign necessary in today's world? And what are the principal forms that redesign is likely to assume?

THE NATURE OF EVOLUTIONARY PROCESS REDESIGN

Surviving in a Shifting Landscape

Beyond all ambitions of growth and development, there is the fundamental constraint and consideration: the company must survive in its industry. This is often a real problem, staring managers in the face as they steer their enterprise through periods of chaos and turbulence.

The survival problematic arises because in many industry branches companies operate in a rapidly changing environment. The operative business environment is complex, not limited to the immediate suppliers, clients, and competitors of the enterprise. The mature enterprise is part of an ever more closely linked industrial, social, cultural, political, and ecological milieu. Whenever any element of this larger system undergoes change, an entire cascade of changes (or "bifurcations") results for the enterprise. Some markets vanish as others open up; established areas of growth and profitability fade while others emerge; current technologies grow obsolete as new ones come on line. Competitive advantage shifts accordingly. A redesign of the structures and functions of the company becomes imperative.

This process can be understood as a shift in the underlying business landscape. A simple topographical model—shown here in Figure 5.1—highlights the relevant factors. We take a two-dimensional plane on which corporations move in horizontal directions. We introduce into this plane a third dimension: that of "fitness," meaning current profitability and competitiveness in the industry sector. Companies can now move also in a third dimension: the higher they climb on a hill, the greater their profitability and the better their competitiveness. How high any given company climbs depends on two factors: the height of its hill (this measures the potential degree of profitability of an industry sector), and its own ability to climb (its level of actual and potential competitiveness).

We must specify that the landscape is not static: the fitness hills are subject to change. Some hills rise, allowing new peaks of profitability and competitiveness; others descend and eventually vanish, squeezing firms out of business. Such changes occur as new players enter the field, markets close or open up, and new technologies and service or product lines emerge and old ones become obsolete.

Managers who note that their company operates on a shrinking hill face the challenge of finding the way down from it, and over to another hill that is less vulnerable and has real growth-potential.

It is instructive to consider how the problem of shifting from one hill to another is solved in nature. In the biological world, entire species and populations can face this challenge. With modifications in climate and in predator or prey populations, environmental niches may change and become unfavorable for survival. At the same time, other survival niches may open up, allowing populations to maintain themselves and even to grow. But living species can seldom manage the feat of leaping from a disappearing fitness hill to a rising one.

Living species other than human beings have a real problem in navigating a changing environment. They cannot look across valleys to neighboring peaks and purposively revise their "adaptive strategies." Instead, they must trust random mutation and natural selection to get them across. This is at best difficult and often impossible. When at the peak of its fitness hill, whatever mutation a species might produce will *reduce* its fitness: at the top of a hill, every road leads down. Mutations in the dominant species constitute alternative evolutionary pathways,

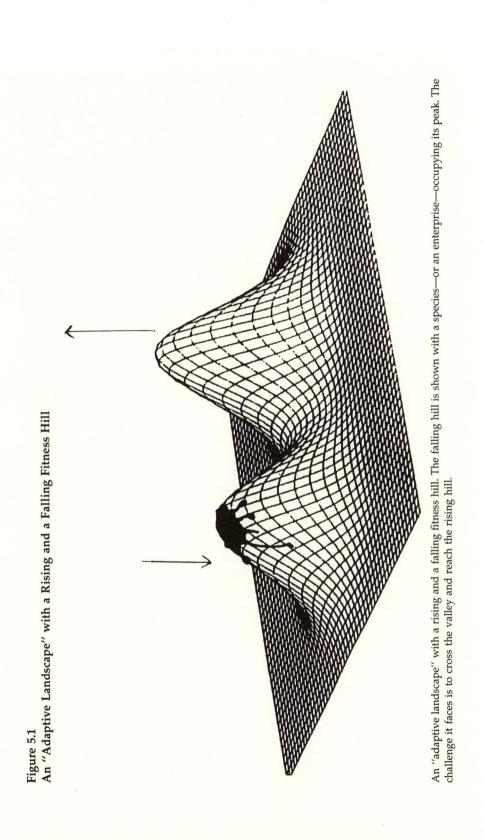

An "adaptive landscape" with a rising and a falling fitness hill. The falling hill is shown with a species—or an enterprise—occupying its peak. The challenge it faces is to cross the valley and reach the rising hill.

and since these mutations occur randomly, there is an overwhelming probability that each of these pathways will be less fit for survival on the existing hill than the dominant type. In the long term, this would not be a problem: the task is to get away from the hill, and that can only be done by climbing down it. However, natural selection acts in the present and does not accept vouchers for the future. Before a mutant could climb down its hill and cross a valley to another, better hill, it will be eliminated by the merciless selection mechanism of nature.

More often than not, an erstwhile dominant species is defeated by the challenge to climb away from its current fitness hill. If that hill keeps shrinking, the population, too, shrinks. And the "hopeful monsters" (as mutants are described by biologists) it produces are eliminated in their capacity of current monsters, regardless of the hope they might embody for the future. Then, when the present hill vanishes, both mainline populations and mutants vanish with it. It is not surprising that the vast majority of the species that have at one time or another populated the earth have now disappeared.

How is it, then, that there are still living species on this earth? The method nature employs in evolution may be merciless, but it is efficient. When a species finds itself on a vanishing fitness hill, it is likely to become extinct. But there are always marginal populations and random mutants down in the valleys, struggling for existence. As new hills rise in the changing landscape, some of these "peripheral isolates" find themselves on rising terrain. They are unexpectedly lifted into prominence, within a newly arising generous niche.

An analogous situation can be found in the world of business. Economic, political, or technological parameters can suddenly favor a hitherto marginal industry or enterprise. In Hungary, for example, under the former socialist regime, there were a handful of private workshops specializing in equipment for ice hockey players. When the government decided that by the first of the following month all motorcyclists in the country must wear safety helmets, these marginal players found themselves rising unexpectedly to prominence. The centralized state industries were unable to meet the demand; only the small private outfits could make safety helmets. In response to the panicky demand by people relying on motorbikes to get to work, they were allowed to put in additional workers and worked day and night to meet the deadline. Later demand settled into a stable pattern, and the newly grown workshops were allowed to satisfy it.

Similar situations arise when any other factor condition changes unexpectedly—new technologies become available, fresh markets open up, and tax provisions and environmental impact quotas shift. Of course, factor conditions can also change in the opposite direction. Formerly big-time players may find themselves squeezed out of the game, and onto steeply descending profitability slopes.

In the natural world, species and populations do not have the advantage of foresight and planning and must trust to blind chance to ensure the fit of their genetic endowments with an available fitness hill. Yet blind chance is extremely time consuming. (For example, to run through all the colored faces of a Rubik's cube, it would take a blind man an average of 126 billion years. This is because his chances, according to astrophysicist Fred Hoyle, are on the order of 1 in 10^{18}, so that if he takes one second for each move, the laws of probability tell us that he would require 126 billion years to complete his task.) Biological evolution does take time—a span of 50 thousand years is short for a new species to emerge. Managers, on the other hand, do not have that kind of search time. Their problems are urgent, and if they rely on random trials and errors, they may be out of business before they get off the ground. Fortunately, they can play a more informed game and thus save considerable time (Hoyle has also shown that a player operating with full and reliable information can unscramble the Rubik's cube in 120 moves, and that, at a second a move, takes two minutes instead of 126 billion years). Managers must play an informed game. They must not lock their enterprises into vanishing market niches and fight disappearing opportunities with obsolete technologies and outmoded organizational structures. They must master the art of climbing down from diminishing hills of profitability and competitiveness and crossing valleys to new and rising slopes.

Staying with the old way of doing things would produce diminishing profits and negative rates of growth, and lead to the displacement of the company by more informed competitors; and looking for new ways by trial and error would take far too long to be of any use. The better alternative is to use evolutionary information to redesign the organization so that it can fit the continuing demand of clients, the changing capacity of suppliers, the rising power of new technologies, and the enhanced competitiveness of rival players on emerging global markets.

Evolutionary Redesign Types

Developing the capacity for evolutionary process redesign is imperative for enterprises, whether they are large or small, long-established or new on the block.

Let us first take a large and established company as an example. Such an enterprise faces the danger of getting stuck in its own rut, and this can be deadly even if its particular rut has been successful in the past. In a changing business environment, the evolutionary management principle "extrapolate the future, not the past" (Op/5) is a precondition of continued success. Implementing this principle takes effort. Past strategies are not easily forgotten when they are reinforced by the inertia of large and already ossified organizational structures. The hierarchic matrix-organization of a large company may follow "tried and tested" practices to the very edge of disaster, and then beyond.

No matter how successful they were in the past, large companies must undertake the exercise of evolutionary redesign if they wish to ensure continued profitability and competitiveness in today's volatile environment. This exercise involves what in Figure 5.2 we call an "organizational bifurcation," that is, the transformation of the organizational matrix from a hierarchic to a heterarchic mold. The transformation is to enable semiautonomous divisions, departments, and teams to make operative decisions, instead of passively implementing preconceived blueprints handed down from headquarters. In other words, the functioning of the organization is to shift from the "centrally programmed" to the "parallel-processing" mode, thereby approximating the flexibly self-stabilizing functions of a cross-catalytic cycle rather than the rigid behavior of a classical mechanism (Principles Org/3 and Org/4). (The case study that follows illustrates some aspects of this challenging task in actual business practice.)

As our second candidate for redesign, we take a medium-sized company. Such a firm faces a different problem. Due to its modest size and limited organizational basis, it may be unable to access the full range of the technologies and information required to remain competitive in global markets, dominated by profit- and market-share-hungry giant companies. If the middle-sized player is not to be acquired by the bigger players (or else, resisting, be pressed into insolvency), it must create cross-catalytic cycles within its own industry sector. Such cycles can be created by bringing together similarly positioned companies in mutual-benefit clusters. For small- and medium-sized companies, participating in these clusters requires evolutionary redesign in the form of another variety of fundamental change process: a so-called "convergent bifurcation" (see Figure 5.3). This is a transformation of the operative modality of the companies, from relatively autarkic to a collaborative mode. It can be achieved through networking, strategic coevolutionary partnerships, and the creation of entire business ecologies by means of production, trade, or marketing clubs, and similar affiliations and associations (Principles S/2 and S/5).

Whether it involves organizational or convergent bifurcation, the redesign of corporate structures and functions needs to observe a few basic rules of thumb.

• Design for the sustainability of the entire industry sector, in addition to the competitiveness of your own enterprise.

Figure 5.2
An Organizational Bifurcation

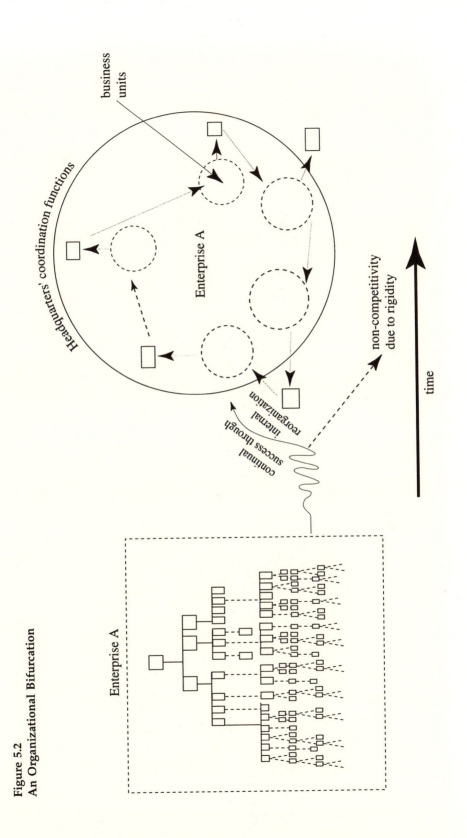

Figure 5.3
Convergent Bifurcations

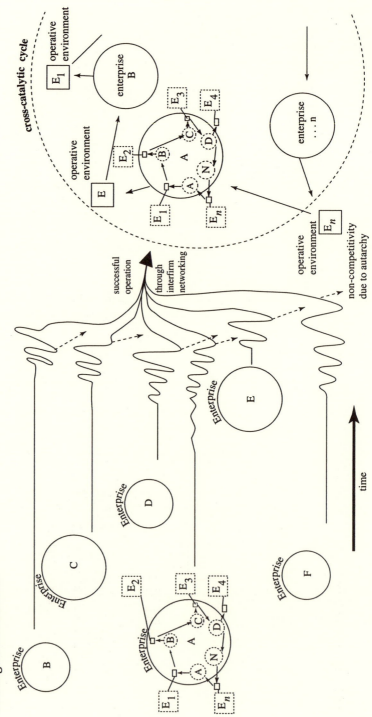

- Facilitate participative management within your company, and share your vision even with your partners and erstwhile competitors.
- Focus on processes and not on structures as sources of competitive advantage.
- Identify sensitive points where small, well-timed inputs can have major and widely spreading consequences.

The advantage of managers of business enterprises over biological species is that in order to maintain a good fit with a changing environment, they are not obliged to rely on mere chance. They can purposively shift organizational modalities as well as product lines, operations, and technologies. Those who achieve familiarity with basic evolutionary trends can use their "business knowledge of the third kind" to keep up with the changing topography of our age of unexpected chaos and accelerating bifurcation.

EVOLUTIONARY REDESIGN IN ACTION: TWO CASES

The basic considerations and typical cases described here can be clothed with detailed substance by taking two cases where evolutionary redesign principles have already been applied in practice. (The case studies described on the following pages come from the work of one us in the Paris-headquartered transnational Lafarge, a "Fortune 500" building materials company.)

Redesign of an Underperformer in a Down-Market

The $250 million southern division of Lafarge Corporation, a billion-dollar U.S. subsidiary of the company then called Lafarge-Coppée, was in poor shape in 1991. With average net losses of over $10 million over the previous five years, it had slipped into an uncompetitive delivered cost position in what was a commodity business. Although essentially single product, the division's business was characterized by many different geographic markets, competitors, and customer groups. Environmental standards and local community concerns were also becoming major factors. Added complexity came from the division's interface with other regional divisions of Lafarge Corporation, with headquarters in Virginia and, as losses mounted, increasingly with world headquarters in Paris.

By the end of 1991, it had become apparent that what was needed was an entire restructuring of the division's activities, including assets and contracts, sales and marketing, distribution, administration, and organization.

Previous efforts to execute effective change had failed for a number of reasons, including lack of capital funds and difficult economic conditions. But the preexisting management methods and style had some limitations as well. Some local decisions had been made with negative consequences for the division as a whole, while some divisional decisions had not taken into account local conditions. Middle and lower managers had been largely eliminated in the process of strategy formulation. An annual planning ritual produced over 200 pages of material, but stifled creativity and action. It also remained far removed from the customer. The complexity of the business had paralyzed decision-making within the existing organizational structure and its mode of operation.

As is often the case with global companies, attempts to resolve the growing impasse took the form of a search for "big maneuvers." The sale or purchase of various $100 million cement plants, which would fundamentally change the division's cost position and market shares, were closely studied, in both Virginia and Paris. Joint ventures and alliances with other global competitors were also sought, as were radical reorganization plans that would have spun off one or more subregional divisions. Because the decision-makers were senior managers from outside the division, their knowledge of what was happening in the field was limited by the number of hierarchical layers and the lack of communication and information exchange between them. As no big maneuvers were implemented, change remained elusive.

An Evolutionary Management Approach

Under a new divisional president, a strategic plan for the division was rapidly put in place. Both its design and execution followed the set of principles described in Chapter 4, consistently with the complex, information-intensive, open, and unstable nature of the division's business. Strategy design involved an active dialogue between cross-disciplinary groups of three or four top managers with the relevant people in the organization: salespeople, terminal managers, plant managers, and divisional headquarters. Front-line employees with customer contact and local operational responsibility were closely involved. During a period of several months, a creative chaos was stirred up, with the motto "consider all alternatives except the status quo." A number of long-awaited actions were implemented to instill credibility in the change program (Principles Org/6 and Org/7).

In the process, the division became more open and outward looking. New partners had emerged, in part because of changing environmental legislation and public expectations. The division moved more firmly into recycling the byproducts of other industries, and became a more integrated building materials company. Ecological constraints and opportunities were addressed head-on, with top managers spending as much as one-third of their time on community, government, and industrial partner relations in this area (Principle Op/3). The role of distribution had also taken on dramatically increased importance, and its function was reorganized to reflect this larger role. With the growth in complexity, there was a greater need to stay sharply focused. The division reasserted its long-term identity as a producer of a low delivered cost commodity product, exiting markets in which it could not be a natural player, and reallocating resources in sales and marketing to target priority customers in priority markets (Principle S/3).

At the same time, divisional management took on a key role in interfacing with Group headquarters because of the competitors, environmental positions, and technologies it shared with other divisions. On as many as five different levels within the organization, the system-within-a-system process of information measurement and control played a key role. In order to achieve effective information management, questions of administration, and measurement and control, were addressed at the executive staff level rather than left to management information systems. By adding dimensions of asset utilization to measures of return-on-sales, the executive staff was able to instill responsibility for asset management into operations, and also gain greater coherence with Group headquarter's evaluation of divisional profitability by return on net assets (Principle S/2).

Results Two Years Later

The process of improvement was not as smooth and obvious as it may seem at first sight. It did, however, yield dramatic changes to the bottom line: 1992 saw losses cut in half, and 1993 has shown a profit for the first time in over ten years. Given the U.S. economy during these two years, with low or zero growth continuing in the southern states, these results can hardly be attributed to external factors. If a rising tide lifts all boats, this change program was executed on the sand banks.

Over a two-year period, the division experienced a net profit improvement in the range of 5–10 percent of sales. Where did these profit improvements come from? While it is impossible to separate gains due to price level improvements from those coming from restructuring or cost reduction, the following sources of profit amelioration can be identified:

- elimination of unprofitable sales accounts
- improvements in product quality
- reduction in plant logistics costs
- optimization of distribution (truck/rail/barge)
- negotiated truck and barge tariffs
- closure of high-cost terminals
- inventory reductions

- better accounts-receivables management
- better product handling in aging plants and terminals
- new products
- plant productivity improvements.

What is significant about this list is the absence of "big maneuvers," and the fact that in itself each improvement represented a relatively small impact, often in the range of U.S. $250,000 to $750,000. The cumulative impact became significant by virtue of the number of actions that were taken.

The participation of large numbers of individuals, and the visibility of direct and quantifiable actions, had a direct impact on the division's identity and culture. Employee morale turned around; customers and competitors understood the division's commitment to its markets; nonperforming assets were clearly identified and are today in the process of being improved or divested. Each manager had a flight plan to which he or she was committed, and the division as a whole had invigorated its identity and acquired a positive vision.

Factors Underlying Successful Change

The success of the program was due to a relatively limited number of key conditions. Personell changes were perhaps the most important—a new president and a new business strategist who shared a vision of change, a majority of line-managers who were given a second chance to be effective, as well as a few who were let go because they did not want to change at all. The seven-member top management team that was formed in the process became central to the program's success, as facilitator and initiator of change rather than as "boss-bossing" decision-maker (Principle Org/1). The executive committee served the 1,000 employees that were running the operations, and not the other way around. In this process, the willingness to throw out conventional ideas and ways of doing things became a paramount factor.

A shared focus on delivered costs became effective only when employees began to understand that top management was serious about "participative management." Suddenly, the president was spending a large amount of his time in informal meetings across the division, sharing his vision, asking what was going on in the minds of front-line employees ("the people who make our business happen"), demanding better performance, and listening to all ideas on how to do it. For the first time, front-line employees were given the power to effect change; their opinions were solicited. As the new business strategist, one of the present authors was spending most of his time in structured meetings with customers and working sessions with line-managers. After the first few months, he began getting phone calls from salespeople from Amarillo, Texas, to Baton Rouge, Lousiana, and West Palm Beach, Florida, with ideas and suggestions that had immediate and significant impact on the bottom line. Was this change due to prior inertia, or lack of responsible management? More likely, the reason was simply that a coherent program of change had never reached those people who were in the best position to make change happen.

A constant search for new products, new services, and new relationships with a growing number of players in the division's business, so as to improve both competitiveness and the competitive dynamics of the industry, also began to yield results once a participative and operations-driven change program was underway.

A third precondition was the making of a goal-oriented information and measurement system. In this division, from strategic plans to sales reports to financial tables, a mix of hard-to-use computer systems, traditional ways of doing things, and lack of direction resulted in hundreds of boxes of reports and printouts every month—a mountain of paper that no one read or used. Even more damaging was the fact that the existing reports hid unprofitable accounts, products, or activities. Salespeople resorted to volume targets, plant foremen to production targets, and distribution managers to throughput targets—with the customer and the division's profit objectives getting lost in the shuffle.

Under the new system, reports and printouts were few in number and simple to use. They forced the measurement of performance in a way that conferred responsibility on the user. Sales reports took the focus away from volume and price, and shifted it to net margins instead, by product, terminal throughput, and territory. Terminal printouts linked inventory levels and product throughputs to net margins. Plant managers were given information about delivered cost competitiveness in the various markets.

The design and dissemination of effective reports was symptomatic, in fact, of a larger information and communications problem. Prior to 1991, the centralized staff functions (accounting, planning, management information systems, and human resources) had been a closed system. Memos were written by staff members to each other, directives were issued to operations, and regular presentations were made to top management. A large degree of insularity had led to one-way flows of information, fostering an attitude of "not my responsibility," and lack of correspondence with the reality of front-line operations. Instead of facilitating the flow of information between operations and corporate management, middle-level managers had largely done the opposite.

The new conditions of operation and decision-making became a motivating force in Lafarge Corporation's southern division within six to nine months. They resulted in a profitability ethic that pervaded every activity. Although the gains that were obtained and projected were not sufficient to meet corporate profitability targets (so that further restructuring and layoffs will undoubtedly be required before shareholder value criteria can be effectively met), the change program which took place between 1991 and 1993 represented a considerable achievement for everyone concerned.

A central theme of this example from Lafarge Corporation is the forcing of turbulent change from within the entire organization. Top management has to create the conditions for instability so that through evolutionary redesign the company could reach new levels of competitivity and profitability. It is only in this way that uncompetitive operations in down-markets can significantly improve performance without waiting passively for improvements in the wider environment.

While every business and business unit has its own problems and challenges in a down-market, all share a growing concern with sustainable profitability. Those that are under-average performers and structurally uncompetitive face a double challenge. In these companies, the principles of evolutionary management have special relevance and utility.

Redesign Following a Critical Socioeconomic Instability

Lafarge's investment in a cement plant in Czechoslovakia in January 1992 represented its first major step into the formerly socialist East Europe (other than the former East Germany, which the Group had already entered in 1990). The investment took the form of a share agreement with the National Property Fund to create a private company out of the formerly state-run cement enterprise. Lafarge's initial minority participation was raised to majority ownership within eighteen months, by which time the French company had become not only financial investor but also the industrial operator of the plant.

Once the core business of cement was secured, Lafarge began a downstream integration into ready-mix concrete. After a year of looking at alternatives, the largest single network of ready-mix plants in the country was signed into existence in January 1994. The investment took the form of a joint venture with the leading Czech road construction company (Stavby silnic a zeleznic a.s.), in which Lafarge contributed know-how and capital, and the Czech company contributed 22 existing ready-mix plants, trucks, and market positions. The new company, operating under the name of Beton Lafarge, made Lafarge instantly one of the leaders in the Czech ready-mix industry.

The next wave of investments for the French group was in specialty products ranging from basic mineral-based mortars to colored organic coatings, building paints, external thermal insulation systems, adhesives, sealants, and concrete admixtures. A first retail store was opened in Prague in May 1994, a second logistics platform in 1995 and a third in 1996, selling a range of specialty products to building professionals. Other products were certified to Czech standards and imported by truckloads from company production centers in France, Germany, and Italy. Still other product areas were developed through commercial joint ventures with Czech producers, much as for Lafarge's refractory products division (October 1994).

Automated production controls were introduced, raw material quality assurance implemented, new concrete formulas made up, worker safety procedures enforced, production equipment recalibrated, and concrete trucks repaired and acquired. As in the case of cement, market forces determined everything from pricing to market shares, investment policies, and employment levels. Once again, there was temptation to engage in short-term thinking both among the newly emerging players and by the individual companies confronting rapid change without firm points of reference.

The Growth of the Specialized Building Material Sector

During much of its 40-year tenure, the communist regime failed to repair or renovate buildings and infrastructures. As a consequence, much of the country's estimated 1.7 billion square meters of external facades and 2 billion square meters of internal wall surfaces have been severely neglected. This means that the potential for mortars, external coatings, internal paints, floor and wall sealants, adhesives, and related products has grown enormously.

In the five years since the revolution, a cautious increase in investments has occurred, to increase the quality and expand the range of available products with special attention to the preservation of the environment. Both the new local producers and the foreign entrants (the latter through imports, capital participation, or acquisition) have been increasing their market share at the expense of former state-owned firms such as Hasit (in mortars, glues, and sealants) and Barvy a Laky (in building paints), although these firms had previously dominated the market. Because of the high-valued-added nature of these products, foreign companies could penetrate Czech industry with imports in a way that has not been possible in cement and in ready-mix.

One of the key difficulties in the specialty products market was educating the customer about cost/benefit tradeoffs between old and new product technologies. Often the user (painter, mason, plumber, tile specialist, etc.) could not contemplate having to pay more for a product that replaced a combination of old technologies even though this brought cost savings and enhanced performance at the system level. As a result, firms, in order to be successful, had to create customer demand through innovative marketing at multiple levels, including distributors, architects, designers, building authorities, applicators, and end-users. Product specification sheets, product demonstrations, direct consultations, free training for applicators, and extensive technical support have been part of the shared investments costs of all the leading players in the specialty building products industry.

The Evolutionary Strategy of Lafarge

It soon became apparent to management that (a) the decisions it would make in the first 12 to 24 months would determine its developmental path thereafter, and (b) its influence as a local industry leader in construction materials would help determine the health and future prosperity of the industry. No rules of behavior had been set; standards of practice were in the process of formation; and management style and culture were still nascent. In such conditions of relative chaos, bifurcation to a new level of operation depended on which actions were initially taken.

One of the first steps taken by management was to establish long-term objectives regarding its target capacities, market shares, pricing, costs, and product range. These objectives, although ultimately driven by profit targets, were grouped around three major axes: the search for improved productivity, the instillation of quality, and respect for the environment.

The objectives were formulated in light of information on competitors, customer demand, norms and standards, and community expectations. An analytic tool known as the "histogram" was drawn up for each local market: this device showed probable delivered costs for all competitors, probable sales by competitor in that market, and price policies by product. Tempered by current practices and apparent behavior, the histograms enabled management to choose objectives that were coherent with the underlying interests of the industry.

The management team itself operated in multiple layers, with ultimate responsibility vested in Munich as headquarters for Central Europe, and extensive support by a development office in Brussels and world headquarters in Paris. During 1992, one of the present authors was appointed general manager of the Lafarge office in Prague, working closely with the management of the acquired cement plant, as well as with local partners (acquired subsidiaries, suppliers, joint venture companies, distributors, law firms, and various specialized consulting firms).

As general manager, this author implemented many of the evolutionary-systems principles described in Chapter 4. To name but the most important: the company's strategy, elaborated between 1990 and 1994, was an exercise in envisaging the future instead of extrapolating its past experiences (Principle Op/5: "Forecast to multiple horizons by extrapolating the future, not the past"). It was fact-based and issue-driven in a context where the company's ability to influence the wider course of events became the key to success. Rather than develop rigid action plans that were then delegated to subordinates, the approach taken was to share the long-term objectives at every level possible and create conditions for productive and motivated work, allowing at the same time a team-driven effort to identify specific opportunities and the policies to be implemented (Principle Org/2: "Support interaction and consensus among teams at all levels of the enterprise"). Linkages between the various construction material activities—primarily cement, concrete, aggregates, building paints, facade mortars, admixtures—were emphasized also in the investment program (Principle Op/2: "Include variety costs and the cost of linkages between activities").

Product quality based on West European norms and standards was anticipated (Principle Op/1: "Anticipate quality through evolutionary dynamics and open-system marketing"), and "ecological" safeguards and investments were immediately put in place (Principle Op/3: "Compute ecological constraints and opportunities and internalize their cost").

Coevolutionary partnerships within the nascent industry took the form of open dialogue with government, communities, suppliers, distributors, architects, and commercial partners in the search for new and sustainable structures to replace the ancient mechanisms. The practice of selectively forgetting the past had relevance at every level, from the manual operations of workers to customer service, accounting methods, law, and corporate strategy. Finally, interfacing with the local cultures required rapid internationalization at the middle and upper levels of management (Principle Org/8: "Globalize the company culture by 'internationalizing' coordinating functions and 'localizing' operating functions").

Several aspects of the cement plant's operations called for close interaction with the local communities, including the reduction and control of noise and fugitive dust in operating the quarry; the reconversion of quarry land to agricultural use; SO_4 and NO_x emissions; reductions in energy consumption; employee layoffs; medical sponsoring; and various other concerns. Direct meetings with the mayors of the communities became a priority in a program to gain their goodwill as active partners for the company.

The creation of Beton Lafarge was a natural extension of the Group's long-term competitive concerns (Principle S/3: "Maintain a consistent long-term competitive focus"). Selecting a strong Czech partner provided a capacity to react within the national context; this would have been absent in a greenfield strategy. The rapid transformation from internal producer of concrete to a service company (Principle S/2: "Continually monitor and adjust strategic positioning within the industry system") geared to external clients required extensive hiring and firing, initially creating a difficult work environment (Principle Org/7: "When radical change is needed, engender transient chaos"). Although stress levels were high during the first six months after the founding of Beton Lafarge, the instability and discontinuous change provided an incentive for attempting dramatic progress.

Although several shortfalls appeared during this first phase, the existence of well-defined objectives, a clear attribution of roles, a realistic compensation plan, and, above all, management's vision of how the company could succeed in the future, provided the coherence necessary to survive (Principle Org/1: "Re-cast leaders as stewards and teachers").

Within the local organization, several key people were recruited, including a Czech general manager who replaced the original general manager in 1995. In early 1993, the new recruit was sent to France for training and acculturation: methods and values at Group headquarters are part of the company profile required for key operating positions. At the cement plant, a top-level human resources manager was hired to oversee the program of restructuring anticipated for the following years. (This was not without considerable difficulty in a country in which functions of human resource development had been largely absent). In reducing the labor force by about 50 percent, the concern was not only efficiency and cost reduction, but also to assure the best possible retraining and indemnification of the employees who were to leave the company. Counseling and post-layoff guidance, as well as unemployment funds and funds for start-up venture assistance, were created.

The long-term objectives and modes of operation were signaled to competitors through a willingness to yield where the underlying economics made sense and a determination to stand strong where they did not. The same held true for customers, suppliers, and other collaborators in the country. The health of the broader industry system was taken into consideration even as continual adjustments and business developments were undertaken (Principles S/2: "Continually monitor and adjust strategic positioning within the industry system," and S/5: "Compete for sustainable industry-level advantage").

By early 1995, effective teams had been established at the cement plant, in the Prague office of Beton Lafarge, and in various subsidiary companies, working in concert toward well-understood objectives. Profitability in 1993 and 1994 was good, although it could have been higher had short-term and self-centered policies been pursued. Constructive relations have developed with local competitors, based on a competitive but nondestructive rivalry. Relations with local communities, suppliers, and distributors have evolved into effective partnerships based on transparency and trust.

After two years, not all the results can be considered positive: problems of land restitution, difficulties in hiring good collaborators, a poor work mentality, recurring disputes with competitors over regional market shares and pricing policies, and a continuing recession in the country continue to weigh on prospects for the future. However, by 1996 the trend for the cement, ready-mix, aggregates, and specialty building materials sector has become one of assured growth and profitability. The outlines of competitor behavior and industry practice have emerged positively out of the period of turbulence that followed the breakdown of the old system in 1989. In all of this, the application of evolutionary management principles made a vital difference.

CONCLUSIONS

In today's low-growth, intensely competitive, fast and turbulent operating environment, successful executives need to adopt a new knowledge base for effective and responsible decisions. Some managers—often the most successful ones, in key positions—already operate with a new approach to key decisions. They develop strategy iteratively within the entire organization instead of top down; they replace the base-case alternative and the "big maneuver" with a number of parallel, well-focused actions; they give priority to developing the ability of the enterprise to learn; and they view the company's operating environment as a complex and dynamic economic, social, and ecological system. These are hallmarks of the new knowledge base required for managing enterprises in the contemporary world, and they are often intuitively attained.

The line of demarcation between the new and the old ways of managing is well-chronicled. Intuitive managers operating in the new way enable their companies to produce rapid growth in profit and market share—for example, Wal-Mart in retail distribution, Lafarge in construction materials, Ford in automotive design, Citicorp in mortgage originations, ABB in power systems, and Matsushita in home products, among others. Executives in these corporations focus less on established structures and more on dynamic processes; they measure the cost of time, information feedback and control, and spend a growing percentage of their time and resources on creating business ecologies through intensifying relationships with suppliers, distributors, competitors, communities, government agencies, subcontractors, as well as with nature. They adjust production and service positioning in search not only of the highest profit margin, but also of sustainability within the industry system, including corporate partners, government, local communities, and the physical and biological environment.

The question is: do today's executives adopt such strategies on the basis of personal intuition and business acumen, or ground them in explicit and reliable knowledge? The answer is by no means clear. Managers often "know" what is right before they can analyze and explain it; consequently they frequently act first and think later. As D. Isenberg noted in an oft-cited article in the *Harvard Business Review*,[1] they develop thought about their companies and organizations not by analyzing a problematic situation and then acting, but by thinking and acting in close concert. This is becoming a risky way of doing business. A penchant for spontaneous acting worked well during stable, continuous growth periods, before globalization, informationalization, and systemic interdependence made a full impact. In the more difficult competitive environment of today, managers who are enduringly successful cannot afford to rely on intuition and acumen alone. While intuition and a good business sense continue to be important assets, only a sound understanding of the processes that define the dynamics of change in the industry—and in the larger system within which the industry and their particular company is positioned—is truly reliable. This means that in today's informationalized and globalized business world, managers must be informed about the properties of complex systems, and the nonlinear dynamic that drives the transformations of these systems. This does not call for becoming an evolutionary systems scientist, but it does call for acquiring the minimum of essential knowledge that constitutes evolutionary literacy. In this book we have attempted to provide the basics of such knowledge.

We hope that this introduction to management based on evolutionary principles will prove to be both useful and illuminating for the reader. It has certainly proven to be such for the writers.

NOTE

1. D. Isenberg, "How Senior Managers Think," *Harvard Business Review* (November/December 1984).

Postscript

A Philosophy for
the Twenty-First Century

THE EVOLUTIONARY VISION

Modern management is not like mathematics—the detached application of rules to clearly contemplated facts. In many cases and situations, it is an instinctive and spontaneous game where implicit images and subconscious background knowledge play a crucial role. Even the comprehension of conscious principles is decisively facilitated or blocked by the features of the background against which they are envisaged. As we already had occasion to remark, managers are often spontaneous players—they do not first think and then act, but think and act in concert. *How* they think when they act spontaneously is important: it determines whether they act successfully or not. Consequently for managers, the subconscious assessment of the situation takes on importance, in addition to the cool and conscious calculation of context, data, and applicable action principles. To some extent, this applies to everyone inside and outside the business world: as the mathematician Poincaré remarked, we all carry a picture of the world in our head. The question is, *what* picture? The answer to that can spell the difference between good decisions and poor ones.

It makes sense, then, to complement our familiarity with the principles of management derived from evolutionary thinking with familiarity with the vision on which that thinking is based. Assimilating the main features of the evolutionary vision can provide managers with the necessary "feel" of the situations they confront in today's rapidly changing business environment.

In this Postscript, we sketch some of the basic characteristics of the vision that underlies what many scientists now regard as "the evolutionary paradigm." This paradigm has important implications not only for management practice, but also for public leadership and business ethics; it is the indicated philosophy for the twenty-first century.[1]

The first thing to note about the evolutionary paradigm is that it does not ask "what a thing is" in and by itself (as the classical paradigm did); it asks "how did that thing (or person, or event) become what it is now?" The noteworthy elements of this world are not what they were created, but what they have *become* in the course of their existence. Becoming is a process of change that never returns to its point of origin: evolutionary development is irreversible. It is also indeterministic. The way a system—be it a human, a society, or an enterprise—evolves is not determined at the outset. Each process of evolutionary change generates its own path, drawing on the integration of many chance factors within an overall developmental path.

The modern evolutionary view of systems reflects a major shift in scientific thinking. Until the dawn of this century, the scientific world picture was highly deterministic: everything that took place occurred as a result of absolute necessity traced to the action of immutable natural laws. The world as a whole resembled a vast mechanism. Not for nothing was Newtonian physics called classical mechanics. Possession of this science enabled Laplace to make his famous reply to Napoleon's query as to the place of God in his system. "Sire," said the great mathematician, "I have no need of that hypothesis." Assuming that his basic premises were correct, Laplace was right. In a deterministic universe, subsequent things follow rigorously from prior things. If you know what came first, you can compute what will come later. But Laplace's deterministic premises were incorrect. Soon they were questioned, and later they were abandoned.

Already in the middle of the nineteenth century, Darwin challenged the reign of determinism in nature by maintaining that, in living species, mutations are random. More than that: in Darwinian biology, random mutations have random interaction with the environment, so that natural selection is based on the workings of twofold chance: on the outcome of random mutation, and on what the mutant happens to encounter in its milieu. This randomness created a split within science. Physics was under the domination of Newtonian determinism; and Bergson, Boltzman, and other great minds of the nineteenth century labored in vain to reestablish consistency. Not until well into our own century could physics and biology be reconciled, and in the process both underwent fundamental change. Physics admitted chance as a basic factor; and biology integrated chance in a sequence of development that has a quasi-deterministic coherence all its own.

The revolution in scientific thinking took off in earnest in mid-century. With the advent of Ludwig von Bertalanffy's general system theory, Ilya

Prigogine's nonequilibrium thermodynamics, Norbert Wiener's cybernetics, Claude Shannon's information theory, Rössler's and Abraham's chaos theory, Benoit Mandelbrot's theory of fractals, and the other "sciences of complexity," the scientific worldview transformed from the machine-like determinism of classical mechanics and the chance-riddled indeterminism of Darwinian biology into the self-consistent universe of evolving dynamical systems.

The concept of evolution emerging from these sciences has hardly anything in common with classical Darwinian notions of life-and-death struggle and nature's merciless selection of the fittest. Conflict and competition do exist in nature as in society, but they are contained within the bounds of larger systems which depend on cooperation and synergy for their existence. Far from the infamous notions of tooth-and-claw struggle to assure the survival of the fittest—"social Darwinist" notions used by Hitler to justify the expansionist politics of national socialism—the new evolutionary sciences point to the logic of coordination and harmonization as the essential context of creative competition.

In the new evolutionary vision, the things of enduring interest are dynamically integrated configurations of matter and energy, consolidated through the exchange and elaboration of information. These are the things that grow and evolve. They are known as dynamical systems, and they exist far from the stable but inert condition of equilibrium. (In equilibrium—and here thermodynamic equilibrium is meant—there are no temperature differences or chemical gradients in a system, everything is uniform. Consequently, no heat can flow, and no irreversible reactions can take place; the system is "dead.") It turned out that the level of evolution of a system, and its distance from equilibrium, are correlated. The further a system evolves, the further it is from thermodynamic equilibrium. For example, an organic molecule is further from equilibrium than a stable atom; a mouse further than an amoeba; and a human being further than a mouse.

The complex structure of highly evolved systems is not held together by the balance of forces within enduring stable structures, but by mutually tuned cycles and feedbacks that respond to each other and compensate for deviations from the system's norms. The kind of balance that occurs within evolving systems is "dynamic" and not "structural." It is not the balance of the Eiffel Tower, where counterposed girders hold up a permanent structure, but the balance of the circus team that forms a human pyramid. Here the muscles of each acrobat constantly monitor and respond to the movement of all the other acrobats, keeping everyone in dynamic balance with everyone else.

But even the human pyramid is a poor example of the balance that occurs in evolving systems. The fact is that evolutionary processes are not oriented to any form of equilibrium, not even a highly dynamic form.

Instead, they are oriented to growth and development. An evolutionary process embraces the destabilization of the structures it has created just as much as their dynamic balancing. The reason is that evolution never takes place within the evolving system alone but always in the context of a finely tuned (and hence unstable) relationship with its environment. No evolving system is an island. A closed system could not endure for long; sooner or later it would use up its energies and "run down." The famous Second Law of Thermodynamics knows no exceptions: whenever a system performs work—does anything at all—it uses up ("down-grades") energy. Its waste energies can never be fully recycled: it would take more energy to lift the waste to the usable level than the system would gain by using it again. This is why there can never be a perpetuum mobile within a closed system.

Although closed systems move inescapably toward the inert state of thermodynamical equilibrium, evolving systems do not. In the course of time, they move irreversibly (but not smoothly and continuously) toward states that are ever more complex, and ever further from equilibrium. They do so by constantly replenishing their stores of matter and energy with fresh energies and resources drawn from their environment. The environment of an evolving system is both the source of fresh matter and fresh energy, and the sink of its waste matter and waste energy. Consequently, evolving systems depend vitally on their milieu.

The more evolved a system, the closer and more sensitive is its coupling with its environment. Environmental coupling, however, is not a static condition but a dynamic mutual balancing act. Conditions in the environment tend to change, and so does the system itself. As a result, there is likely to be a constant series of fluctuations testing the flexibility of the system/environment interface. Normally, a system balances any deviation from its normal environmental interactions, positioning itself so as to obtain the resources it needs and to discharge the wastes it generates. But for many systems a time comes when this balancing act can no longer be performed. When that happens, the system either collapses or it restructures itself. The human pyramid collapses and dissolves into individual acrobats. An organism, an ecology, or a society can do better: it can restructure itself. The process tends to be nonlinear; it creates a break with what went on before. Systems in the real world evolve through the alternation of extended periods of dynamical self-stabilization with short periods of revolutionary restructuration. The rhythm of evolution is like the life of the small-town policeman: it consists of long periods of boredom interspersed with short periods of terror.

These concepts tell us something about the world in which we live. Evolutionary restructuration is in full swing—not, of course, in individual human beings whose organism is defined by the genetic code, unalterable during a lifetime, but in society. A human society is not genetically but culturally coded. Society's codes are mores, values, customs, practices, laws, regulations, and the like. At all times, and especially in periods of stress and crisis, these can and do change. As a result, human society, and within it community, culture, social and political organization, and business enterprise, tend to evolve. Individuals with fixed genetic codes in their bodies enter and leave these groups, but the groups themselves are time and again restructured by new "cultural" codes.

Extended self-stabilization, periodic instability, and a leap to a new form of stability: these are the critical benchmarks of the evolutionary process. Whoever views the world in these terms sees it differently from those who view it in light of the classical conceptions of stable structures, linear development, and temporary deviation from equilibrium.

Unfortunately, today's leadership thinking still persists in mechanistic and equilibrium-oriented modes. Conservative executives analyze political systems, enterprises, and markets as if they were machines that can be taken apart and fixed. They seek to identify the malfunctioning part in order to repair or replace it. They view fluctuations as a threat, and deviations as actual danger. The standard aim is the maintenance or reestablishment of the past state of the system—the "law and order" of a regime or the equilibrium of a market.

Traditional leaders intervene to reestablish the status quo. In the business sphere, they fight competition and legislation and, if need be, fire and replace personnel. In the political realm, they mobilize public opinion and, if pressed, call up the police or the armed forces. Such actions disregard that when human groups encounter a basic instability they cannot be returned to the status quo. As do other evolving systems, societies, cultures, communities, and enterprises restructure themselves to new levels and forms of dynamic equilibrium. It is pointless to intervene in this process with a view to returning the system to its previous states. When mergers or acquisitions change the structure and function of a corporation, it can be no more returned to its previous operating modalities than the international community can be returned to the bipolar world order after the dissolution of the socialist system and the disappearance of the Soviet Union. Yet uninformed managers try time and time again to reestablish the equilibria of "tried and tested" structures in their enterprise, just as the Pentagon has been trying to reestablish a world order dominated by military might even if it is exercised by one superpower rather than two. Such attempts are mostly in vain. Their results are bound to be partial and transient, whether they occur in international affairs or in business.

In the final count, the selection of the vision through which we view the world is not an idle exercise in conceptual gymnastics but a major determinant of decision-making. There is no rational decision uninformed by worldview, just as there is no seeing and hearing uninformed by cultural conditioning and social experience. The "forget-the-theory, let's-get-down-to-action" pragmatist is not efficient; he is only naive, and hence a poor decision-maker.

EVOLUTIONARY LEADERSHIP

The evolutionary vision is effective whether it concerns the world of business or the business of the world. It offers a powerful way to look at business and at the world at large—a way that can promote responsible approaches to political and business leadership.

Pioneer evolutionary scientist Erich Jartsch noted that the reward for the elaboration of this vision will not only be an improved academic understanding of how we are interconnected with evolutionary dynamics at all levels of reality, but also an immensely practical philosophy to guide us in a time of creative instability and major restructuring of the human world.[2] One of the present authors ended his 1987 book *Evolution: The Grand Synthesis* by noting that by becoming conscious of evolution we can make evolution conscious—and by conscious evolution we can defuse threats and promote the creation of more mature, more autonomous, and more dynamically stable human systems.[3] That same author published in 1991 *The New Evolutionary Paradigm*, in which social psychologist David Loye outlined the expected benefits of the development of a natural-science-based evolutionary transformation theory in regard to society.[4]

For effective and responsible leadership, the principal benefits are as follows.

1. The benefits of improved forecasting. While the study of evolution through chaos in the natural sciences has uncovered specific limits for predictability during transitional states, it is now also discovering new possibilities for improving forecasting within these limits by identifying patterns that foreshadow either impending chaos or potential order out of chaos. The new advances suggest how more effective early warning systems may be developed for identifying impending food, financial, political, and environmental crises. The need for such systems became crystal clear when, basically unprepared, the leaders of the international community faced the great waves of system transformation that began in mid-century with decolonization in the Third World, continued in the 1980s with glasnost, and led to the series of near-miss crises in 1991 that included war in the Persian Gulf, and a coup followed by dissolution in the Soviet Union.

2. The benefits of improved interventional guides. As important for effective leadership as the improved forecasting of impending crises and transformations is the identification of fruitful routes that could lead *out* of the crises. Indeed, one of the greatest problems faced by leaders today is in knowing where, when, and how to intervene either to prevent social, economic, political, or ecological crises or, if prevention is no longer possible, how to alleviate and ultimately overcome the crises. The evolutionary vision holds out an important promise in this regard: mathematically formulated dynamical systems theories allow the creation of computer graphics that makes it possible to reduce vast quantities of otherwise confusing data into comprehensible form. This can simplify the comprehension and communication of problems and the visualization of swift and effective intervention strategies. In view of these capacities, dynamical systems theorist Ralph Abraham believes that evolutionary modeling—especially in the form known as modular dynamics—can provide contemporary civilization the means to transcend its coming crises.

3. *The benefits of participatory rather than authoritarian problem solutions.* The traditional recipe during times of trouble has been to turn to specialized experts for advice and to implement the advice through top-down authoritarian strategies. As the eventful history of Eastern Europe since 1989 has shown, attempted solutions that disregard the participation and motivation of the wider masses, whose life and well-being are affected, exacerbate the problems they were meant to solve and create a new range of difficulties. The promise of the evolutionary vision in this regard is that it permits the sharing of the concept underlying proposed problem solutions by broad segments of the population. If they would forget the technicalities that generate the computer models, and communicate instead the basic, and basically simple, vision that generates even the technicalities, leaders could ensure the wide level of public comprehension that is the precondition of the success of their strategies.

4. *The benefits of providing clearer long-term goals and humanistic images.* Futurists and social scientists have remarked that, in contrast to the fervent visions of a better future that animated the revolutions and reforms of the eighteenth and nineteenth centuries, in the present century a confused and fearful humanity seems to be running out of positive vision. Romantic utopias have been dismissed as unscientific, the Marxist vision has failed, and visions inspired by religious tenets seem too otherworldly to motivate practical strategies. The utility of the evolutionary vision includes the promise of rectifying this situation. Thanks to this vision, we can now begin to grasp in a dependable scientific way not only the vacillation of systems and societies around their already-established traditional states, but also their breakthrough to new evolutionary states that open a full range of fresh possibilities. By this token, the evolutionary vision could revitalize currently atrophying images of the future and

positively recharge public motivation in reaching for long-term objectives that are humanistic in intent and realistic in attainment.

EVOLUTIONARY MANAGEMENT ETHICS

The evolutionary vision is a vision inspired by science, but it does not enjoy "scientific neutrality"—no theory or vision originating in science and having to do with human affairs does; scientific neutrality of this kind is a fiction. It is simply not true that science applied to human concerns is only about facts and has nothing to say about values. In regard to the contemporary world, for example, whoever truly knows the facts knows that this is a world in rapid and critical transformation, and also knows that this transformation can be consciously and purposively steered. He or she cannot remain neutral in possession of this knowledge.

When managers acquire a scientific perspective on the contemporary world, they can remain neutral least of all—they are the class of decision-makers with the greatest steering power, and hence with the greatest responsibility for steering. They must recognize that the world of business must be linked with science not only in connection with the application of scientific knowledge through technology, but also in regard to responsible thinking and decisions. The problem of our time is not the technical mastery of nature, but the mastery of the forces released through science and technology for human ends.

Responding to the problem of our time calls for responsible behavior. Responsible behavior is practical ethics: the translation of sound principles into action. This is part of the morality that underlies all intercourse in society. As the human individual matures, his or her experience becomes infused with social overtones. Instinctive socialization is the foundation of life in a community; it is the primary basis of society. Without some form of social morality no society could be maintained, or could even come into being.

In the evolutionary view, human society is not the outcome of a dispassionate contract between people to cooperate in the pursuit of shared goals—Rousseau and other "social contract" theorists went overboard in their rationalizations. Rather, society is an evolutionary emergent. As individuals interact in a shared milieu, their autocatalytic cycles interlock in cross-catalytic hypercycles; patterns of mutually supporting behavior develop. This reinforces natural empathies and gives rise to synergistic convergence on the level of the group, the next level of social organization. Primary groups in turn cross-catalyze among themselves and then with higher-order groups, forming the many layers and structures of modern societies. In the process, social morality becomes codified: first in taboos, mores, and rites, and later in systems of unwritten and written laws. Morality assumes the form of ethics, a set of principles to which reflective people who share a moral conviction may subscribe.

Unlike instinctive morality, ethics is a rational and conscious attempt
to formulate the principles of good and bad, right and wrong. Compared
with morality, it has the advantage of being open to scrutiny, reflection,
and improvement. This is important, because codes of behavior need to
be periodically adjusted, brought level with the evolution of society. Today's ethics are not exempt from this rule. The collectivist ethics of Marxist socialism has collapsed, and religious ethics has a limited hold in civil
society. The ethics associated with traditional value systems seems des-
tined to disappear, while the dominant individualistic ethics of industrial
society has been essentially unchanged since its formulation 200 years
ago—it is still primarily focused on the problems and preoccupations of
the first industrial revolution. It seems time to catalyze a conscious innovation at the leading edge of contemporary society: time for a new
leadership ethics, above all, for a new management ethics. Before closing
this philosophical postscript, we shall outline the main concept of such
an ethics.

We begin by noting that the "soft" factors that were long neglected
by "hard-nosed" analysts can no longer be ignored; they are an essential
element of the new management ethics. The valuation of people is the
foundation. This valuation must be embedded in the evolutionary context: life is not only living, but the chance of its perpetuation. A genuine
respect for living entails a respect for the chances of life of the next
generations. A concern for society must be complemented by a concern
for the future.

The valuation of people calls first of all for valuing one's collaborators.
Genuine human resource development is an integral element of the new
ethics, in the enlightened interest of the enterprise itself. The "soft culture" already growing in innovative enterprises needs to be purposively
nurtured. After all, the interests of individuals, of the organization in
which they participate, and of the society that is their shared environment, coincide. A recognition of this coincidence can generate enormous
energies. No longer need people be divided by incompatible goals in
their private and in their professional life; they could identify themselves
with their organization and fulfill both themselves and their professional
duties.

When the professional and the personal spheres come together within
a complete identity, individuals are not deprived of freedom and pri-
vacy; on the contrary, they see themselves as part of a meaningful corporate community to which they contribute through work that is both
their livelihood and their personal interest.

In the mature systemic enterprise, people have not only professional
but also brain and heart qualifications: they not only *know* what they are
doing, they also *understand* and *like* doing it. Einstein's dictum is much
to the point: you cannot solve a problem with the kind of thinking that
gave rise to it. The problem of work motivation and ethics cannot be

solved with the kind of thinking that led to their near-demise. That kind of thinking considered work as a necessary evil—something one had to do, if one were to make a living. But the eight-to-five workday in an impersonal work environment is a European invention of the eighteenth century. Except for slave labor and forced labor intended as a punishment, it did not exist in other cultures and at other times. In so-called primitive cultures, people seldom worked for more than three or four hours a day, and in many cultures (notably among Latin people) work is still performed only to the extent that it is required to keep body and soul together. Although the idea of working "in a job" has now spread throughout the world, as that world transits into the postindustrial mode it is becoming increasingly counterfunctional. It is high time to eliminate it from the current and coming corporate reality.

The eight-hour workday and forty-hour workweek is already fading into history. With it must fade the mechanical compulsion to do work independent of personal motivation and interest. Mediocre work performance, especially when interfaced with powerful information-processing systems, can lead to serious misjudgments and major, perhaps catastrophic, consequences. Routine work in the prescribed job needs to be replaced by flexible and creative work that people perform with expertise as well as with ambition. When people are fulfilled they have ambition, motivation, and creativity, and these are the human ingredients of corporate success.

While managers need no longer manage workers in the traditional sense, they do need to make sure that in their organization people and tasks are well matched for abilities, ambitions, and temperaments. They must also see to it that people have the information they need to perform their tasks expertly as well as willingly. They must ensure that on no level of employment is work either meaningless or incapable of supporting the worker. Satisfying this responsibility is good ethics and good management: the simplest of tasks has a bearing on the success of the enterprise. If all persons in the organization become aware of their contribution to the whole, they can find meaning in their job and motivation to do it well.

The ethics of work itself needs to be reconsidered. Ambitious people live to work, while people in routine jobs just work to live. Neither the one nor the other satisfies today's requirement. Working and living are mutually supporting enterprises, inseparable and symmetrical but never unilaterally dominant. To work is neither just to "make a living" nor is it the very substance of living. Work is no more but certainly no less meaningful than any other area of human activity, from family relations to education, culture, sports, and hobbies. Each area of activity intersects with all others and jointly forms the hypercycles that maintain society, and all the groups and subsystems within society.

Remaining at the leading edge requires not only empowering and motivating the workforce, it also means reorganizing the workplace. In a poorly structured organization, even a high level of work motivation will soon dissipate. A workplace organized as an inflexible hierarchy is economically and socially unviable. Dedicated workers who understand both *what* they are doing and *why* they are doing it need scope to exercise the creativity spurred by their dedication. They require a flexible, network-like organization where they can provide inputs to the best of their insight and ability.

Evolutionary managers need to evaluate themselves as well. Leadership in today's world calls for integrated and multifaceted personalities, able to see themselves and to act in the inseparable interest of self and business, and business and society. For this reason, managers must find a balance between the rational, the emotional, the sensual, and the spiritual dimensions of their personality. A simplistic separation of mind from body—the same as that of the private from the business sphere—is not sufficient. In any case, the separation between the professional and the private spheres is breaking down. The work of managers enters their private life, as well as the private life of a great many others. And people's private life shapes the way they work.

The rhythms of change in our unstable world are penetrating the world of business. The managers of the new generation, now moving into positions of leadership, question established values, attitudes, and practices, and search for new ways of thinking and acting. They could—and indeed should—realize that they are a critical part in a vast evolutionary process. As a result they need to combine effectiveness with responsibility. They need to be concerned not only with the immediate profit and growth of their corporation, but also with the natural and the social environment in which it operates, and with the personality and fulfillment of the people who work for it.

The urgently needed management ethics is an evolutionary ethics. Its features reflect the features of the evolutionary process itself: this ethics is open, interactive, and embracing of the coevolution of individual and enterprise, enterprise and industry sector, industry sector and nature, and nature and society, and therefore of individual and the emerging global socioeconomic system. Tunnel vision and myopia do not dissolve the bonds between business, society, and nature; they only create shocks and surprises.

Promoting the evolution of the economic, social, and ecological environment in which their enterprise operates is in the direct interest of management, the same as promoting the innermost sphere of their collaborators' vision, motivation, and personality.

NOTES

1. For further details, see Ervin Laszlo, *The Systems View of the World* (Cresskill, N.J.: Hampton Press, 1996).
2. Erich Jartsch, ed., *The Evolutionary Vision*, CAAAS Selected Symposium #61 (Boulder, Colo.: Westview Press, 1981).
3. Ervin Laszlo, *Evolution: The Grand Synthesis* (Boston and London: Shambhala, 1987); reissued in an updated and enlarged edition as *Evolution: The General Theory* (Cresskill, N.J.: Hampton Press, 1996).
4. David Loye, "Chaos and Transformation: Implications of Nonequilibrium Theory for Social Science and Society," in E. Laszlo, ed., *The New Evolutionary Paradigm* (New York: Gordon and Breach, 1991).

Appendix

Notes for the Technically Minded

NOTES ON THE ENTERPRISE

Informationalization

In the past, societies have been mainly shaped by information processed in human brains. This was the case when it came to raising children, creating businesses, setting up local or national governments, organizing churches or armies, and founding schools or theaters. But in the course of the twentieth century, the information processed in human brains has been more and more supplemented by information processed in technical systems. In the last decade of this century, businesses operate not only in a social but also in an informational environment. Human societies have become more than social systems: they have turned into socio-technological information-processing systems.

A Historical Retrospective

The "informationalization" of society began in antiquity, even if it has vastly accelerated in our time. The inventions of the number system, of the alphabet, and of money itself were already major information-processing innovations. The abacus, a uniquely simple and useful calculating machine still used in Russia and in the Orient, is 3,000 years old. In antiquity there were also some mechanical contraptions that extended human computational powers, but machines that would significantly improve these powers by executing calculations through built-in programs appeared only in the seventeenth century. In 1642 Blaise Pascal invented an adding machine that may have been the first digital calculator, and in 1671 Leibniz created an instrument that multiplied by repeatedly adding. In 1833, Babbage produced the Analytical Engine and created a logistical basis for building genuine computing machines.

It was about 100 years ago that information-processing technologies took off. Herman Hollerith succeeded in the automation of the U.S. census count at the end of the nineteenth century, and Bell invented the telephone. At around the same time, Hertz developed the principle of wireless communication and pioneered the development of radio. Konrad Zuse built his Z1, Z2, and Z3 computers in the 1930s; and Eckert, Mauchly, and Goldstein created the cumbersome but already accomplished ENIAC computer in 1946. UNIVAC I, a vast machine with 5,000 heat-generating vacuum tubes taking up an area of 220 square feet and weighing five tons, was used in 1952 to predict the landslide victory of Dwight Eisenhower. It made a sensation on national television.

The invention of the computational architecture of digital data processing by mathematician John von Neumann permitted a quantum leap in electronic information processing. Through digitalization, numbers, letters, words, sounds, images, and the measurement of mechanical and electrical instruments could be rapidly and accurately transformed into strings of electronic pulses. Digital signal-processing computers became commercially available in the early 1950s, benefiting from the concurrent mass production of transistors for hearing aids and radios. In the 1960s, computers entered the field of production. CIM (computer-integrated manufacturing) harnessed the new-found powers of the digital computer to integrate the different elements of manufacturing, so that the entire process could be operated as a single system. By virtue of the unique capabilities of the computer, this system could be flexibly automated and operated on-line, in real time.

In the 1970s, the development and implementation of the full capacities of CIM made slow progress, since most companies applied computer technology to the automation of isolated elements of manufacturing, creating "islands of automation" with little integration of the bits and pieces within an adaptively optimizing manufacturing system. But by the 1980s the situation changed: major manufacturing enterprises became aware of the competitive advantage of overall automation, optimization, and integration in a total-system process of manufacturing. The leading-edge industries began to encompass in computer integration not only the technological elements of the manufacturing system—product design, production planning and control, and shop-floor automation—but also such managerial elements as strategic planning, finance, human resources, and marketing. This, as the trend depicted in Figure A.1 indicates, has resulted in the coming of age of the computer-integrated manufacturing enterprise.

Figure A.1
The Increasing "Informationalization" of Activities and Processes in the Modern Enterprise

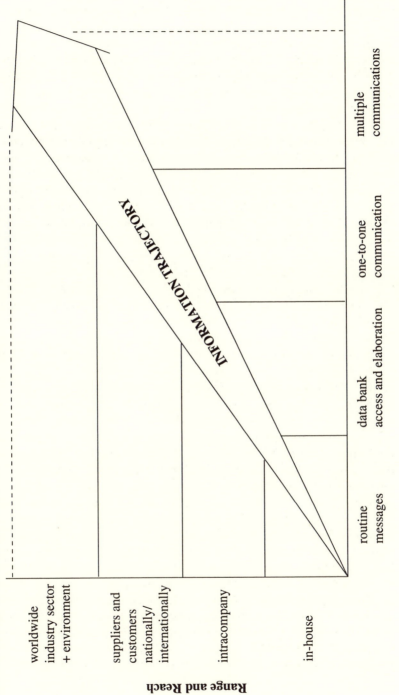

INFORMATION TRAJECTORY

Range and Reach

worldwide
industry sector
+ environment

suppliers and
customers
nationally/
internationally

intracompany

in-house

routine
messages

data bank
access and elaboration

one-to-one
communication

multiple
communications

Form and Type

The managerial applications of computers were accelerated by the availability of mass-produced table-top workstations. In the 1980s, the power of the already super-powerful mainframe systems of the 1970s was successfully compressed into workstations that could be readily accommodated on individual desks. The table-top units were interconnected through a variety of methods and technologies, and the resulting distributed computing environments allowed individuals to reach out from their personal computers to networks and mainframe or special-purpose computers.

Cognitive processes are now progressively transferred to computers. The storage and processing of information by computers, together with the new technologies of telecommunication, is creating vast networks that gather, process, store, and transfer information without requiring (or even allowing) operational intervention by humans. Such systems are deeply embedded in the structures of modern societies and interact with them in countless ways. Global manufacturing companies, and international banks and financial institutions, have almost completely delegated their financial routines to computer programs integrated within worldwide telecommunication networks. Information processing systems are thoroughly integrated in manufacturing (CIM), in design (CAD), and in inventory control (Just-in-Time systems). They perform essential functions for the military (Early Warning and remote sensing systems), in telecommunications (communication satellites), in ground and air transportation (automatic rail switching systems, autopilots, and instrument landing systems), and in such complex operations as balancing the atomic chain reactions of nuclear power stations.

Information has also become the crucial factor in channeling flows of capital. As Walter Wriston, long-time head of Citicorp, indicated, the information standard has replaced the gold standard as the basis for international finance. Worldwide communications enable and ensure that money moves anywhere around the globe, in answer to the latest information, or misinformation.

By the 1990s, thousands of complex operations have been programmed into computers as algorithms and, in artificial intelligence, as sophisticated heuristics. The market for computers—laptops, desktops, workstations, minis, superminis, mainframes, and supers—attained more than U.S.$220 billion. For the past several years, there has been an estimated 10 percent annual decrease in size of system per unit of performance and another 10 percent decrease in cost. Because the learning curve does not show signs of leveling off, more and more information-processing systems are likely to come on line in coming years. A new "nervous system" is evolving in societies. It integrates technological systems and human beings with complex mutual feedback loops, and stores information in ways that are far more permanent and of several dimensions larger than any form of information storage used in previous societies.

Current Developments and Impact

It is estimated that more than 90 percent of all the scientific-technological research and development ever undertaken occurred in the period since the beginning of World War II. The technologies that came on line did more than achieve linear improvements in quality, quantity, speed, and reliability—they depart radically from classical industrial technologies. For effective utilization, the new information-based technologies require new work habits, new consumer patterns, and new forms of social and economic organization.

The latest advance is hallmarked by the shift to knowledge-based technologies. In the past, the automobile, the airplane, and the electrical and pharmaceutical industries among others evolved out of traditional craftsmanship and practical experience. In contrast, the emerging industries of the late twentieth century owe their existence to the integration of knowledge and the results of scientific research. On the one hand, advances are occurring beyond the scope of scientific research, involving knowledge-integration through novel modes of configuration and system-building. Management information systems (MIS), for example, are defined as much by their networked systems characteristics as by the hardware and software they use. On the other hand, there are advances based directly on the commercialization of scientific R&D. This is the case in industries as diverse as microelectronics, bio- and genetic-engineering, artificial intelligence, new materials, waste management, and communication. Because of the latest shift to knowledge-based applications, process logistics and whole-factory productivity management are replacing the application of labor and raw material to individual branches and mechanisms. The university-trained "knowledge-worker" is replacing the traditional apprentice who depended on work-experience to acquire the necessary skills.

The operative environment of contemporary business is shaped by advances in information-processing capacity in the new computer hardware and software; by progress in knowledge configuration and integration; and by the business impact of research in sciences such as high energy and quantum physics, physical chemistry, molecular biology, genetics, as well as nonlinear logic, AI, computer science, and cellular automata theory.

The new advances in knowledge create a fast-changing and complex foundation for corporate activity. They highlight the importance of sound management decisions for the effective use of the available information. To extract benefit from a potentially useful item is both complex and costly. It is not enough to access the raw data; management also has to have the capacity to cope with what it accesses. To develop and even to maintain the required information-processing capacity calls for highly developed human resources, a proper organizational structure, and sufficient capital. In the United States, in the period 1929–1982, increases in output per worker were due 64 percent to advances in technology, and fully 30 percent to worker education. Keeping up with requirements in these areas requires considerable investment. In Japan, for example, since 1986 R&D spending has exceeded capital spending in 50 percent of the top industrial companies. This is for good reason: in the industry branches where the top Japanese companies operate, information is by far the major cost and labor factor. The material cost of an electronic chip is only 2 percent of its total production cost, and seldom requires more than 6 percent of the workforce of a company.

Globalization

Interdependence and internationalization were among the catchwords of the 1970s and 1980s; globalization is the catchword of the 1990s. There are good reasons for this: fundamental processes have now reached a critical threshold; and these processes drive people and societies into ever more, and ever closer, forms of cooperation and association with each other. Technology and business are among the foremost actors in this process, which is itself a feature of the evolutionary gigatrend.

A Retrospective on Globalization

The roots of the modern corporation reach back to the "corps do métier," which were small guilds that emerged in France and elsewhere in Europe in the twelfth century. From these modest local beginnings, corporations have grown into their contemporary mold, expanding in size, complexity, range of activity, as well as geographic and market penetration.

Until the nineteenth century, the size, market span, and complexity of business firms were limited by technology, transportation, slow economic growth, and the widespread use of barter instead of money in agrarian societies that had a predominantly feudal structure. Even where markets emerged on capitalist principles, the main beneficiaries were merchants, bankers, warehousekeepers, and maritime agents; production itself was limited largely to artisanal workshops. Where there were concentrations of industry, they took the form of federations of workshops loosely bound by shared raw materials and labor pools, and connected by common seaways or riverways—the Rhine, the Baltic, the Meuse, the Bay of Biscay, and others. The only commercial enterprises that employed large numbers of workers were the mines. As early as 1550, some

European mines had up to 12,000 workers, working not only under the surface, but also as water pumpers, transport entrepreneurs, and suppliers of food and clothes. Since no single owner could finance operations on such a scale, mining stocks were divided into shares (Kuxen). For the rest, medieval firms were small, and they centered on the figure of a single owner.

According to French historian Hubert Bourgin, economic activity between the fifteenth and the eighteenth centuries was exercized mainly by firms of one of four kinds. One kind were small family workshops including a master-tradesman, two or three journeymen, and one or two apprentices. Another kind included a group of workshops of similar size, but connected to each other through supplies, labor, or market logistics, often through the person of the ruling merchant. The third kind of firm included enterprises of somewhat larger dimension: these were the "concentrated manufactures" made up principally of breweries, tanneries, glassworks, and textiles, assembled with a more advanced division of labor under the roof of a large building. Only the fourth kind of late medieval firm presaged the industrial enterprises of the nineteenth and twentieth centuries: these were companies building ships or manufacturing, among other things, paper, swords, and wire, with the use of mechanical saws, cranes, and hydraulic wheels. Some of these companies emerged already in the sixteenth century, but few were significantly mechanized until the nineteenth.

In the eighteenth and especially in the nineteenth century, the established manufacturing enterprises benefited from the coming of age of mass production and the intensifying flow of migrant labor from the countryside to the cities, where impoverished peasants were forced to accept employment for survival wages. The new "industrial proletariat" was treated as an unreliable and often troublesome (but cheap) appendage to machines, with which it was to be replaced whenever possible. Supplied with cheap labor, and driven by a series of breakthroughs in the technologies of mass production—the Bessemer steel process, the rotary kiln in cement production, the mechanical loom in textile weaving, and the traction-based combustion engine in transportation, among others—manufacturing companies soon grew in size, complexity, and market span. They transformed from owner-based workshops into professional manager-headed hierarchical organizations. Their specialized workforces drew on economies of scale and enabled them to reach a growing array of markets.

Most of the familiar giants of industry—including the U.S. automotive "big three," as well as General Electric, Westinghouse, the Bell Telephone System, together with Japanese transportation and heavy industry companies such as the Mitsubishi Group, French cement producers such as Lafarge, and German high-technology firms such as Siemens and chem-

ical companies such as Hoechst—were established well before 1914. Although they operated in the context of a world wreaked by two world
wars, they managed to adapt from peaceful to wartime production, frequently benefiting more from contracts with embattled governments
than from civilian orders in times of peace.

Following the end of World War II, the major manufacturing firms
embarked on another dimension of growth: toward internationalization.
The confluence of production, commerce, the technologies of control and
information, and the changing political scene provided leading businesses with both the opportunity and the means to span the world. In
search of profits and competitive advantage, and driven by the constant
series of technological innovations, manufacturing giants went first international, and then global.

In the immediate postwar years, GM, Ford, and Chrysler were among
the U.S. companies that pioneered the leap from the national to the international level. Their initial motivation was the search for profits,
where the driver was the low cost of overseas labor. But in the process
American manufacturing companies transferred considerable know-how
and technology to the new host countries. Before long, domestic industries arose in Europe and Asia, as well as in Latin America. Some of
them, in Europe and later also in Japan, caught up with their U.S. counterparts in regard to competitiveness and profitability. For example,
while U.S. companies were still seeking cheap labor offshore, Japanese
firms were investing in global market shares, using low discount rates
to build low-cost positions based on economies of scale. In the automobile industry, the doubling of cumulative production in the manufacture of combustion engines led to some 20 percent reduction in direct
unit costs. In addition, large-scale production brought premiums in both
quality and price. Expanding into more and more related product
branches, Japanese manufacturers, such as Honda, Nissan, and Toyota,
became industry leaders.

U.S. firms fought valiantly with the new Asian competition through
large capital investitures to build ever larger operations: the largest factories, the longest product runs, the most intense marketing campaigns,
the strongest sales forces. But, as industry analysts later realized, just as
U.S. corporations were beginning to exploit the economies of scale, experience, and technology, Japanese companies undertook further innovations. These included flexible manufacturing systems, total customer
responsiveness (TSR), total quality control (TQC), and constant differ-
entiation and automation, among others. Through such strategies, Japanese corporations could meet customer demand with minimal delay and
at lowest cost. By learning to cope with diversity—larger customer and
broader geographic portfolios, more product introductions, wider product range and manufacturing process of any given set of resources—

these companies propelled entire industry sectors along the path to full-fledged globalization.

Of course, whether American or Japanese, not every industry could reap full benefits from global reach. Some were inherently local, because of service content, diseconomies of scale, or costly geographic product differences. But most industries have been able to benefit at some level of activity, for example, R&D, raw material sourcing, or overheads. And globalization has reduced certain areas of risk, such as earnings fluctuations in specific geographic markets.

In recent years, the intensifying IT environment has become a major driver of the globalization process. Because information can spread rapidly from company to company, it had become more difficult to build competitive advantage through the commercialization of inventions. In the early part of the century, research and development of new products led to profitable leadership positions that could be conserved first through patents and later through famous brand names (Ford and Ivory Soap are good examples). But when the knowledge base of innovation became globally and almost instantly accessible, imitation had quickly led to the dissipation of profits in new projects. French television manufacturers were leaders in the development of top-of-the-line models with soft touch and remote control, coming out with these features well ahead of their Japanese counterparts. But because the Japanese were able to take over this new technology and produce improved products in a very short time, the success and payback for French manufacturers remained low. By the mid-1980s, the largest French television producer was in serious difficulty and considered selling out to one of the Japanese electronics firms.

As a result of the shortened invention–imitation–dissipation cycle, many firms have shied away from risky upstream sources of competitive advantage and have turned to new forms of growth. On the one hand, companies moved further downstream into consumer and service areas; on the other hand, they expanded horizontally, through mergers and acquisitions. Government deregulation (beginning with relaxation of antitrust enforcement under the Reagan administration and the reduction of protective industry barriers in the European Single Act), as well as tax rate differentials across countries have been further drivers toward increasing size and horizontal expansion.

The creation of multinational companies constituted one stage in the growth-wave of business; the next stage was the emergence of *transna*tional, that is, genuinely global, corporations. The multinational giants of the 1960s treated foreign operations as distant appendages for the production of goods designed, engineered, sold, and serviced in their home country. The chain of command in a multinational was clearly linked to nationality. But, by the late 1980s, no country was holding a

monopoly on technology, capital, talent, and innovation. In the continued search for profit and growth, internationally operating companies
went transnational. The most sophisticated among them made breakthroughs in the laboratories of one country, placed shares with investors
from others, and put the nationals of still others on a fast track to the
top.

The wave of acquisitions and mergers in the 1980s, and various innovative forms of strategic alliances in the early 1990s, turned many a
"niche player" into a national and then into a global player. The latter
learned to rely on cash-flow calculations rather than on national loyalties
to decide where to shift production and capital. Unlike the multination-
als that maintained fiefdoms in different countries that paid dividends
to the national headquarters, today's decentralized global players or-
chestrate the efforts of national subsidiaries in consideration of the
worldwide marketplace.

Japanese businesspeople reckon that by the early twenty-first century,
no more than five global players will dominate the world market in
practically every industry sector. Whether this will come to pass or not,
it is evident that even in such a growth-field as the airline industry—
where, according to the U.S. Department of Transportation, the number
of passenger miles is expected to double to 214 billion by the year 2000—
the elite circle of global companies is becoming ever smaller. No more
than twelve global carriers will emerge by the end of the decade, in the
estimation of British Airways Chairman Sir Colin Marshall, while other
industry analysts estimate only half as many; the remaining 150 international carriers will be limited to national, regional, or niche markets.

Intensifying global competition impels even middle-sized companies
to leap from the national to the transnational level. Many come together
through innovative networks and associations among themselves. The
fact is that national firms either branch out, tap international markets
and create international economies of scale, or risk being swallowed up
by the globalized giants. In the retail food sector, for example, 50 global
companies account for 75 percent of total purchases in Europe. There are
an additional 500 national-level enterprises that seek entry into the European single market in order to remain competitive. They fear becoming
targeted by the Europe-wide players—many of them are already on the
shopping lists of the latter. The global companies themselves expand
aggressively: industry leader Nestlé, for example, bought out Rowntree,
Sooner Snacks, Tom's Food, and Thomi & Franck in Great Britain; Bui-
toni and King's in Italy; Benedict, Heimb's, and Zoegas in Germany;
Sanpareil in Belgium; and Granja Castello in Spain—all since 1988. To
avoid a similar fate, a number of national companies, including Markant
in Holland and in Switzerland, Socadip in France, ZEV in Austria, Selex
in Spain and in Italy, and Linda-a-Velha in Portugal joined together in

August 1991 in an innovative network called European Marketing and Distribution (EMD) with headquarters in "neutral" (non-Community member) Switzerland. With a joint turnover that has reached 82 billion German marks by January 1992 and is growing rapidly, the organization protects its members from untimely takeovers from the industry giants. It is "transnationalizing"—if not immediately globalizing—dozens of previously middle-sized national firms in its particular business sector.

The leap to the global level is leading to the geographic decentralization of sales. Already in 1990, 36 global corporations with a minimum of $3 billion in annual sales made 50 percent or more of their sales in countries outside their national origins, and five of these companies (Nestlé, Sandoz, Hoffman-La Roche, SKF, and Philips) had more than 90 percent of their sales in foreign markets. The foreign sales component has been increasing in most of the multinational players, even if in the majority of them national sales still remain above the 50 percent mark. This has led to, among other things, the local diversification of product lines, but also to some brand names becoming household words in markets where their appeal derives from company prestige and promotion rather than the meaningfulness of the brand name. (Italian housewives ask for Dash, known locally as "Dush," while women shop for Lovable—pronounced "Luvableh"—lingerie in Finland.)

Global companies do not manage their subsidiaries as foreign appendages to the national headquarters: many shift their divisional headquarters to foreign soil. In the late 1970s, NCR was among the first to shift responsibilities for some of its divisions from the United States to Germany. The headquarters decentralization process came into full swing a decade later, when Du Pont shifted its Lycra business operations to Switzerland, Cadbury moved its beverages division to the United States, and Hewlett Packard transferred its headquarters for desktop PCs to France. In 1990 Du Pont also moved its agricultural products division to Switzerland and, in 1992, its electronics division to Japan. In the same year IBM, the traditionally U.S.-based electronics giant, transferred its networking systems headquarters to the United Kingdom, while Hyundai established its PC headquarters in the United States.

The globalization of manufacturing enterprises is matched by the globalization of trade and service companies. In almost all sectors, direct investment across national borders is rapidly on the rise. Driven by the globalization of the leading companies, competitive shakeouts in various sectors, persisting tax and labor-cost advantages, and the need to avoid protectionist sanctions, the cash flowing from one country to another has been increasing by more than 30 percent annually.

In 1994, the globalization process produced another quantum leap: mergers have returned to the business world in a big way. During the first half of that year, there were 2,045 mergers worth $84.4 billion, involving industries such as health care, defense, financial services, the information superhighway, as well as automobile parts. Unlike in the 1980s, when mergers were driven by financial engineering and visions of corporate grandeur, the leap in the mid-1990s has been a direct manifestation of globalization, and the new conditions of competition and the rationalization entailed by it. Competition has become global and tougher, and to cope with it managers have begun to seek a form of rationalization that they can best achieve through intercompany consolidation.

The Power of Global Players

The wealth acquired by global companies represents an unprecedented source of power in the contemporary world. The concentration of wealth, originating in the postwar years, has been vastly accelerating in the last quarter of this century. In 1976, the revenues of the world's largest 200 manufacturing companies equalled about one-sixth of the world's gross domestic product. By 1988, the same share of world GDP was concentrated in the largest 100 companies, and by 1993, only 70 companies made up the corresponding amount. In that year, the "Global Top 5" (Itochu, Mitsui, Mitsubishi Corp., Sumitomo, and Marubeni) generated about 4 percent of the world's economic output.

Global players are eroding the economic sovereignty of contemporary states. National governments do not even know how to consider transnational corporations, much less how to regulate them. It is not clear what national obligations are applicable to a global company, and which nation controls the technology it has developed. It is also unclear how its operations should be accounted. If a U.S. company makes TV sets in Japan and sells them in the United States, should its sales be counted as a U.S. trade deficit in the same way as products made in Japan by Japanese companies and sold in the United States? The governments of even the richest states are often compelled to court the leading global companies, hoping to ensure that some of the hundreds of billions of dollars they invest across national borders would flow into their own economies.

The power of corporations can be matched against the power of nations by comparing the value of sales with that of gross domestic product—convenient although somewhat simplistic measures of economic power. In these terms, business companies are steadily outdistancing entire national economies. In 1993, the combined revenue of the largest three companies surpassed Brazil's gross domestic product, and the revenues of the five largest corporations exceeded the combined GDP of India and China (reaching to U.S.$829 billion as compared with U.S.$774 billion).

Sales as a measure of economic power does not tell the whole story: effective power through competitive advantage can often accrue to smaller, more nimble players. This is true even in basic manufacturing industries where economies of scale are clearly identifiable. In the steel industry, for example, mini-mills such as Nucor and Chaparral have dramatically outpaced larger and more traditional mills, such as USX and LTV.

The economic power of corporations may also be assessed in terms of net profit, on the basis of reinvestable income as well as sustainability. In 1993, the ten most profitable corporations in the world (Exxon, Royal Dutch/Shell, GE, AT&T, Philip Morris, HSBC Holdings, British Telecom, Ford Motor, GM, and Sears Roebuck) had a combined net profit of U.S.$35 billion, which was roughly equal to the gross *revenue* of a country like Hungary. And, while the GDP of an industrializing country such as Brazil has almost reached the combined revenues of the top three global corporations, the heavy indebtedness and public deficits of that country have compared poorly with the profitability and the balance sheets of the global players.

In terms of value-added, which may be seen as yet another measure of corporate power, the leading industrial and service companies may not be chalking up significant gains. The requirement for flexibility and customer responsiveness has led to a broad-based deintegration by shifting operations to subcontractors. Experience has shown that corporations that contract out the manufacturing and service functions not immediately related to their core businesses tend to grow in sales and profits, even if they shrink in value-added output.

However, global companies, with factories, service branches, or sales and marketing organization in many countries, wield a more fuzzy but no less effective form of power: in many direct and indirect ways, they influence the way business is conducted across the world. At the governmental level, decisions involving several countries call for complex negotiations that are often difficult to enforce; while in the business world, corporations create effective multicountry standards and procedures directly as a result of companywide policy. Although corporations number tens or, in a few cases, some hundreds of thousands of employees, while governments claim to represent all the millions of their people, corporations often control crucial sectors of the world economy with far more strategic impact on both nature and society than the public sector.

The effective power of global corporations has kept pace with the growth of their wealth and their geographic span. Through investments, companies transform the fabric of society, influencing lifestyles, employment opportunities, and the balance between urban and rural environments. The decisions of executives affect not only their own businesses, but the lives and environments of the communities where their businesses operate. In many cases, corporate impacts extend beyond the local communities to entire world regions. Responsible credit and investment policies open new paths of development to vast populations, while risky technologies and insufficient safeguards degrade the environment and impair the health of millions.

By creating employment, companies influence the distribution of wealth and create social stability; by bringing value-added products and services to the marketplace, they raise the material standard of living. The roughly 37,000 transnationals operating today, with their more than 200,000 foreign affiliates and 73 million employees, have become the most decisive factor in the complex equation that governs the development of the economies of nations, and the well-being of vast strata of the population.

Systemic Properties

An informationalized global enterprise exhibits properties that distinguish it from other enterprises as well as from earlier stages of its own evolution. We list these properties in Figure A.2 and describe them under a handful of basic headings.

Self-learning, self-organization, and nonsummativity. Whether at the level of a marketing team, a business unit, or an entire industry, every activity innovates and self-organizes in ways which cannot be reduced to its constituent parts. At each point in time, the activity performs differently and involves a different level of complexity. As noted above, diversification and information-intensity are historical trends. The capacity for each activity to continue self-learning depends therefore on whether or not organizational processes and shared values can integrate increased diversity and information flows. Multidivisional, global corporations develop successful learning cultures (Merck, ABB, Komatsu, Lafarge) or risk falling into stasis and decline (IBM, General Motors, Sears, Blue Circle). In each case, success or failure cannot be attributed singly or in a simple sum to the market, the industry structure, the company's management, or its operations. Instead, as we have seen in Chapter 2, the presence or absence of auto- and cross-catalytic cycles explains the capacity of corporations for self-learning and self-organization.

The priority of process over structure. Historically, flows of material and information in the corporation were seen to be determined by the structure of its organization. In matrix models, purchasing, R&D, marketing, etc., were viewed as stand-alone entities which "received" the product or service in an unfinished state, added value to it, and "delivered" it to the next entity. Such structure separation occurred even at very fine levels, within manufacturing or services. In dynamically complex enterprises, however, the *processes* of receiving and delivering play a critical role in cost minimization and customer satisfaction. Delays at each level reduce the firm's ability to deliver the product or service competitively;

Figure A.2
Contrasts between the Properties of the Matrix and the Mature Organization

The Matrix Organization	The Mature Organization
The organization as a whole is the sum of its various activities and strategic business units.	The organization integrates its activities and units in a systemic whole with irreducible properties.
The dominant organizational modality is the matrix hierarchy operated by top-down commands.	The dominant modality of organization is the multilevel heterarchy linked by cross-catalytic cycles.
The development of the various activities and business units is governed by instructions from headquarters.	Each business unit is empowered to learn and evolve its own activities in coordination with all other units within the organization.
Change in the organization is assumed to be linear and predictable and controllable by fiat.	The contours of organizational change are recognized as occasionally strongly nonlinear and in detail unpredictable, even if essentially governable.
The boundaries between the organization and its industry, social, and natural environment are sharp and not readily penetrable.	The environmental boundaries of the organization are fuzzy and penetrable by information and traversed by multiple functional linkages.
Relations between the organization and its suppliers, distributors, and competitors is of the zero-sum "I win—you lose" type.	Relations between the organization and its industry sector are generally of the positive sum "I win—you win" type.
The organization's primary objective is to maximize profit and market share; questions of corporate culture, identity, and meaningful activity are secondary.	Primary goals center on sustainable success through co-worker, shareholder, and consumer satisfaction through conscious concern with corporate culture, identity, and the meaningfulness of business activity.

they also increase the time period of the required forecasting. Increased forecasting horizons mean increased errors and higher inventory costs. The availability of sophisticated information technology (computers + telecommunications + software + information stores) allows companies to engineer processes with very short transfer times between activities, and to bundle activities together such that costs are minimized at the system level.

The prevalence of nonlinear probabilistic change. The evolution of the state of the corporation is constant but not continuous; it is progressive but not linear. As noted in Chapter 2, from time to time management has to make crucial decisions—for example, to break into new markets with new products or services, to refinance part or all of the operations, or to reorganize the corporate structure itself. These constitute bifurcations in the corporation's evolutionary trajectory: they are triggered by instabilities and produce phases of chaos. Managing these processes calls for permitting the self-learning potentials inherent in the organization to come into play by developing several small, parallel, well-focused actions, each with some probability of success. One or more of these actions will then nucleate and produce large, enduring benefits. Japanese companies are often cited for managing product innovation strategy in this way.

Fuzzy boundaries. Due to increasing geographic span, technology control, consumption of limited natural resources, and pollution of land, air, and water, the corporation finds itself interacting with the ecosystem and society in ways that are determinant of competitive advantage and sustainable profitability. Noncompliance with ecology legislation and regulation leads to fines, loss of permits, lawsuits, and in some cases prison sentences for individual managers. On the other hand, ecology-linked products and services may lead to increased sales, increased stock valuation, and decreased government regulation. In this way, the corporation finds itself progressively integrated as a part of its physical environment. A growing parallel trend exists between the corporation and society through its interactions with culture, education, and other quality-of-life factors. Within the business realm, mergers, acquisitions, strategic partnerships, informal networks, minority shareholding, and other modes of interaction between the corporation and other players are effacing the distinction between the company and its competitive environment.

Convergence through alliances and partnerships. The evolutionary meaning of mergers, acquisitions, strategic partnerships, informal networks, and other modes of interaction between the enterprise and external players is convergence to higher organizational levels. The coordinated functions of the merged, acquired, or networked units are hypercycles that integrate the manifold operations of the enterprises on the level of regional, national, or global industry systems. The results are typically lower unit costs or more profitable price levels due to scale, simplification, pooled resources, and industry rationalization.

NOTES ON THE NEW SCIENCES

The New Science of Evolution

In the context of the contemporary natural sciences, evolution is not just the evolution of species, as it was for Darwin and nineteenth-century biologists. Physical nature evolves, too, from the "Big Bang" some 15 billion years ago to the complex and varied phenomenon that now meets our eye. Society evolves as well—from the basic hunting-gathering tribes of the Stone Age to the informationalized and globalized structures of modern societies. These processes follow a common logic: the interactive dynamics that shapes systems as they interact, interpenetrate, integrate, and form new systems on higher levels.

In the last few years, the scientific basis of this process began to emerge with remarkable clarity. Although the final word has not been spoken—in science, it never is—we can already sketch out the most basic and pertinent features of what we can justifiably call "the new science of evolution."

Systems in the Third State

Physics tells us that systems in the real world exist in one of three kinds of states.[1] Of the three, one is radically different from classical conceptions: it is the state far from thermal and chemical equilibrium. The other two states are those in which the systems are either *in* equilibrium or *near* it. In a state of equilibrium, energy and matter flows have eliminated differences in temperature and concentration; the elements of the system are unordered in a random mix, and the system itself is homogeneous and dynamically inert. The second state differs only slightly from the first: in systems near equilibrium, there are small differences in temperature and concentration; the internal structure is not random, and the system is not inert. Such systems will tend to move toward equilibrium as soon as the constraints that keep them in nonequilibrium are removed. For systems of this kind, equilibrium remains the "attractor" which it reaches when the forward and reverse reactions compensate one another statistically, so that there is no longer any overall variation in the concentrations (a result known as the law of mass action, or Guldberg and Waage's law). The elimination of differences between concentrations corresponds to chemical equilibrium, just as uniformity of temperature corresponds to thermal equilibrium. Thermodynamics further tells us that while in a state of nonequilibrium, systems perform work and therefore produce entropy, at equilibrium no further work is performed and entropy production ceases.[2]

The third possible state of real-world systems is the state far from thermal and chemical equilibrium. Systems in this state are nonlinear and occasionally indeterminate. They do not tend toward minimum free energy and maximum entropy but may amplify certain fluctuations and evolve toward a new and more dynamic regime that is radically different from states at or near equilibrium.

How systems can actually become more dynamic in the course of time has long puzzled scientists. The famous Second Law of classical thermodynamics states that in any isolated system organization and structure tend to disappear, to be replaced by uniformity and randomness. Any system that performs work, whether it is a cell, an organism, an ecology, or a society, dissipates its free energy and, unless it replenishes its energy stores, is bound to run down. This is true also of machines—

they always need to be refueled to keep running—and may be true of the universe as a whole, in the event that it is heading toward an ultimate state of "heat death." But it is *not* true of systems that evolve in the universe. These systems are neither isolated nor closed: they are open to inflows and outflows of energy, and often also to flows of matter and information. Consequently, the Second Law does not fully describe what takes place in evolving systems—more precisely, between them and their environment. Although internal processes within the systems do obey the Second Law (free energy, once expended, is unavailable to perform further work), energy available to perform further work is "imported" by these systems from their environment. They have a transport of free energy—negative entropy—across their boundaries.[3] When the free energy within the system and the free energy transported across the system boundaries from the environment balance and offset each other, the systems are in a steady-state. Since in a dynamic environment the two terms seldom precisely balance over any extended period of time, real-world systems tend to fluctuate around their steady-states rather than settle into them without variation.

The Environment of Third-State Systems

Open systems in the third state evolve in all domains of the natural world, in the physical universe as in the world of the living, but they always require a specific kind of environment. This is essentially a flow-environment, in which a rich and constant source of energy irradiates the systems. It is known that such a flow passing through complex systems drives them toward states characterized by higher levels of free energy and lower specific entropy. Already in 1968, experiments conducted by biologist Harold Morowitz demonstrated that a flow of energy passing through a complex molecular structure organizes its components to access, use, and store increasing quantities of free energy.[4] The explanation of this phenomenon in thermodynamic terms was given by Israeli thermodynamicist Aharon Katchalsky in 1971: he showed that increasing energy penetration always drives systems consisting of a large number of diffusely coupled nonlinear elements into states of increasing non-equilibrium. Laboratory experiments have demonstrated the details of the process. They range from the creation of simple Bénard cells in a liquid, to the emergence of life itself in the biosphere.

The Bénard-cell experiment is simple. A vertical temperature gradient is created in a liquid by heating its lower surface. Thereby a continuous heat flux moves from the bottom toward the top. When the gradient reaches a critical value, the state of the liquid in which heat is conveyed upwards by conduction becomes unstable. A convection flow is created, increasing the rate of heat transfer. The flow is in the form of a complex spatial organization of the molecules in the liquid: moving coherently, they form hexagonal cells of a specific size.[5] The cells maintain themselves in the heat flow and dissipate entropy at a high rate. This is radically different from the processes that occur in systems in states close to equilibrium.

Wherever there is an enduring energy flow in a medium, new orders arise spontaneously. This is true of the flow of heat from the center of a star such as the sun to its outer layers: the flow is self-organizing and produces the typical Bénard cells. It is also true of the flow of warm air from the surface of the earth toward outer space. The earth, warmed by the sun, heats the air from below while outer space, much colder, absorbs heat from the top layers of the atmosphere. As the lower layer of the atmosphere rises and the upper layer drops, circulation vortices are created. They take the shape of Bénard cells. Closely packed hexagonal lattices, such cells leave their imprint on the pattern of sand dunes in the desert and on the pattern of snowfields in the arctic. They represent a basic form of the kind of order that emerges in open systems when they move into states far from thermodynamic equilibrium.[6]

Life on this planet may be due to just such a process of progressive organization in third-state systems embedded in a rich energy-flow environment. It is well known that steady irradiation by energy from the sun was instrumental in catalyzing the basic reactions which led to the first proto-organisms in shallow primeval seas. It is also possible that the energy of the earth itself has played a role, in the form of hot submarine springs in the Archaean oceans. The hypothesis calls for a series of relatively small continuous-flow reactors, similar to the chemical reaction systems responsible for Bénard cells. Nature's reaction systems may have consisted of cracking fronts in the submarine rock, causing sea water to heat rapidly and to react with chemicals in the rock and in the surrounding sea. As the hot fluid rose toward the surface, it dissipated its heat. The chemicals that served as the basic building blocks of life were constantly mixed in the continuous flux of energy in shallow seas created by magma erupting into the sea bottom and reinforcing the energy of the sun. Out of these series of reactions could have come the proto-bionts—the lipid vesicles from which the more complex forms of life evolved in subsequent eons.

The Higher Rungs of Complexity

Systems with ordered structure and behavior emerge when sets of reactants are exposed to a rich and enduring energy flow. If the process endures, the systems become increasingly structured and complex. Because they move ever further from equilibrium, they also become more unstable. Their persistence is then due to the catalytic cycles that evolve among their principal components and subsystems.

Complex systems in nature almost always exhibit some variety of catalytic cycles. These cycles tend to be selected in the course of time by virtue of their remarkable stability under a wide range of conditions. They turn out to have great resilience and fast reaction rates.[7] In 1931, Lars Onsager could show that in a steady-state system, cyclic matter-energy flows are likely to arise. For example, in a simple chemical system composed of three types of molecules, A, B, and C, in which both forward and reverse reactions are possible (e.g., $A \leftrightarrow B$, $B \leftrightarrow C$, $C \leftrightarrow A$), the introduction of a continuous energy irradiation into one of the cycles (e.g., $A + hv \rightarrow B$) tends to move the system into a cyclic pattern ($A \rightarrow B \rightarrow C \rightarrow A$). In relatively simple chemical systems, autocatalytic reactions tend to dominate; while in more complex processes, characteristic of living phenomena, entire chains of cross-catalytic cycles appear. Physicists Manfred Eigen and Peter Schuster demonstrated that catalytic cycles underlie the stability of the sequence of nucleic acids that code the structure of living organisms and assure the persistence of the many forms of life on this planet.

Given sufficient time, and an enduring energy flow acting on organized systems within permissible parameters of intensity, temperature, and concentration, the basic catalytic cycles tend to interlock in so-called "hypercycles." These are cycles that maintain two or more dynamic systems in a shared environment through coordinated functions. For example, nucleic acid molecules carry the information needed to reproduce themselves as well as an enzyme. The enzyme catalyzes the production of another nucleic acid molecule, which in turn reproduces itself plus another enzyme. The loop may involve a large number of elements; ultimately it closes in on itself, forming a cross-catalytic hypercycle remarkable for its fast reaction rates and stability under a variety of conditions (cf. Figure 3.5).

The formation of hypercycles allows dynamic systems to emerge on successively higher levels of organization. The shift from level to level of organization through catalytic hypercycles produces the convergent aspect of the evolutionary gigatrend. Convergent systems on successively higher levels of organization have a wider range of possibilities to set forth the process by which they access, use, and retain increasing amounts of free energies in correspondingly complex structures. The reason is that on the new level, the amount of complexity that can be developed in a system is greater than on lower levels, due to the greater diversity and richness of the components and subsystems. The wider range of structural possibilities offers fresh opportunities of evolution. Molecules built of many atoms and cells built of many molecules can evolve toward the complex polymers that are the basis of life; living organisms based on many cells can evolve toward the higher forms of life; and local ecologies based on many species and populations can build toward mature regional and continental ecosystems. Human societies themselves, built of many populations and levels of organization, tend to evolve toward progressively more embracing units: nations and regional communities of nations, and ultimately a global community of all nations and peoples.

Although not smooth and rigorously predictable, evolution moves along recognizable pathways. Even if it contains many leaps, stagnations, and temporary reversals, its overall course produces an envelope that has a definite, and statistically irreversible, direction. We get a basic developmental vector in nature. We can define it as $S^{el}/dt = > 0 \, (\Psi, I)$. That is, the evolutionary level of a system (S^{el}) over time (dt) has a positive (generally increasing) value with regard to the factors Ψ and I. Here Ψ is the degree of entropy-dissipation by the system (which is the amount of free energy per unit of mass processed by it), and I stands for the number of different components whose interactions have a functional role in the system.

These quantities are measurable for many kinds of systems, from atoms to complex organisms and ecologies. Their measurement for human social systems is more difficult, for it involves complex problems in establishing the societal equivalents of physical processes. However, it is clear that the rate of free energy converted into entropy by a system grows generally proportionately to the evolutionary level a system has attained: for example, as cell metabolism is a thermodynamic developmental process, we can say that a mouse dissipates more entropy than an amoeba, and a human being more than a mouse. Thanks to the complex brains of humans, technological societies could transfer entropy production outside the biological organism and increase it beyond its limits: now it is the technologies that we use that convert vast additional amounts of free energy and dissipate more entropy.

Information content is likewise measurable, for example, as the number of bits that are required to construct the structure of a system from its components, or the length of the program that is required to assemble it. Also this parameter grows generally proportionately to evolutionary level: the DNA of a mouse has a higher information content than the single-cell structure of the amoeba, and the DNA of a human organism has more information content than that of a mouse. (If we measure information content by the complexity of the actual organism—the phenotype rather than the genotype—we can add the scale of evolutionary complexification of the neural nets in the brain.) And modern societies bring together complex human individuals within sociotechnical structures that add a whole new dimension of information content to the system.

The combination of entropy dissipation and information content produces a systematic increase in the effectiveness and efficiency with which an evolving system uses the resources available in its environment. (As

we have already noted, in the thermodynamic framework these resources are measured in terms of negative entropy: usable free energy.
The actual use of these energies enables the system to offset the entropy
it produces by performing work with negative entropy. If the rate of
negative entropy import exceeds the rate of positive entropy production,
the system not only maintains itself in its environment but grows and
develops.) Effectiveness and efficiency are driven to progressively higher
levels since the amount of negative entropy available in the environment
of a system is an independent parameter: it is not controlled by the system. Consequently, a system can increase its negative entropy import
only by effectively tapping more sources of environmental free energy,
or by more efficiently exploiting the existing sources. Thus there is a
correlation of evolutionary level, on the one hand, with environmental
sensitivity (the ability to locate and access the various sources of negen-
tropy in the milieu), and, on the other hand, with increases in the density
of the energy flux that is being accessed. (Energy flux density is the
measure of the free energy used—accessed, stored, or converted—by the
system per unit of time per unit of mass: for example, erg/second/
gram.)

Consequently, modern technological societies are not accidental byproducts of a developmental process, but are mainline elements of evolutionary development. They are capable of an increasingly fine
resolution of the relevant features of the environment as well as of the
effective utilization of the selected features. The shift from one type of
technology to another is irreversible precisely because it either permits
accessing some hitherto untapped resource, or it improves the efficiency
with which a given resource is exploited. The technologies of the first
industrial revolution excelled in the former: they tapped the free energies
of oil, coal, and natural gas, the fossil fuels available in the planetary
environment. The technologies of the second industrial revolution now
excel in the latter: they increase the flux-density of the actually used
resources by making each unit of energy do more work.

In light of these fundamental parametric changes, evolution is coherent
and consistent whether it takes place in the cosmos, in the biosphere, or
in society. We humans emerge as highly evolved organic systems, with
significant powers of discrimination of the relevant features of our environment; and the societies we form turn out to be logical extensions
of the evolutionary process: they increase entropy dissipation and information content by adding entire new dimensions to the human powers
of biospheric resource discrimination and exploitation.

The challenge, of course, is to keep these processes from exceeding the
bounds that define the capacity of the global system to support, at an
adequate standard of life, all the humans that are coming into this world.

Chaos Models in Economics

Economists have been interested in modeling complex systems dynamics for over half a century, beginning with the work of Frisch, Lundberg, and Samuelson. They used difference equations, differential equations, and mixed models to generate deterministic paths. For example, the simplest sort of difference equation is the first-order linear equation:

$$y1 = ay0,\ y2 = ay1 = a2y0,\ \text{or}\ yt = aty0.$$

Here, any negative value of parameter a results in an oscillatory time path. However, the primary applications of such models were in macroeconomics (e.g., Samuelson's multiplier-accelerator model); and insofar as complex systems modeling is concerned, it has become clear that such linear models were capable of generating only four types of time paths:

1. oscillatory and stable (converging with oscillations of decreasing amplitude toward some fixed equilibrium value)

2. oscillatory and explosive (cycles of ever-increasing amplitude)

3. non-oscillatory and stable

4. non-oscillatory and explosive.

It was not until the application of nonlinear mathematical models that economics was able to model complex cycles with irregularities not contained in the above four linear variants. However, even with the advent of nonlinear mathematical modeling, economists tended to concern themselves with cyclical time paths rather than oscillatory time paths. By cyclical, we mean a time path, yt, characterized by a cycle whose duration is p periods if it always replicates itself *precisely* every p periods from any initial point in its trajectory. This is contrasted with an oscillatory time path, which is defined more vaguely as one having "frequent" rises and declines in the values of its variables, but in which the time path may rarely or never replicate an earlier point of its trajectory. It is this latter nonlinear modeling which can yield extremely complex time paths simulating chaos. Intertemporal behavior can acquire an appearance of disturbance by random shocks and can undergo violent, abrupt qualitative changes, either with the passage of time or with small changes in the parameters. Chaotic time paths can have the following attributes, among others:

- a trajectory (time path) can sometimes display sharp qualitative changes in behavior, like those we associate with large random disturbances
- a trajectory is sometimes extremely sensitive to microscopic changes in the values of the parameters—a change, say, in the fifth decimal place of one of the parameters can completely transform the qualitative character of the trajectory.
- the trajectory may never return to *any* point it had previously traversed, but display in a bounded region an oscillatory pattern which is consequently highly unpredictable.

The following simple nonlinear one-variable difference equation of the first order can be used to demonstrate chaos dynamics:

(1) $y_{t+1} = f(y_t) = wy_t(1-y_t)$, where $dy_t + 1/dy = w(1-2y_t)$.

The phase diagram in Figure A.3 shows the generation of the time path graphically, for a value of $w = 3.5$. There are four general cases for the phase diagram.

1. If $w < 1$ the phase curve will lie entirely below the 45 degree ray, but if $w > 1$ there will be an intersection point E between the phase trajectory and the 45 degree line.
2. If $1 < w < 2$, the phase curve's slope at the intersection point will be positive.
3. If $2 < w < 3$, that slope will be negative only between 0 and -1.
4. If $w > 3$ the slope will be less than -1.

It is the fourth variant ($w > 3$) which is of interest to chaos phenomena. As in the case in Figure A.3, such a mapped trajectory will be explosive for low initial values of y, followed by cobweb-like oscillations around point E. At the point at which the trajectory encounters the negative slope of the diagram, the oscillations "explode"; as soon as the positive slope is encountered, the oscillations "dampen." For the parametric value $w = 3.5$, these oscillations will involve a rise and a fall in every two successive periods.

A chaos-type trajectory is generated by increasing the value of w to a critical point at which an infinite number of cycle lengths is generated. To see this, we begin with the value $w = 3$. It is *exactly* at this point that the equilibrium point E becomes unstable, because the slope of the phase curve is < -1. Exactly at that value of w, the stable two-period limit cycle makes its appearance. The reader may draw phase curves that intersect the 45 degree line for various slope values, and then generate a time path from a point similar to $y(0)$ in Figure A.3.

As w increases further (to $w = 3.4495$ in this case), a stable four-period

Figure A.3
Phase Diagram of a System Approaching Chaos (Phase diagram based on the equation $y(t+1) = 3.5\ y(\ )/1-y(t)/$, $y(0) = 0.034$)

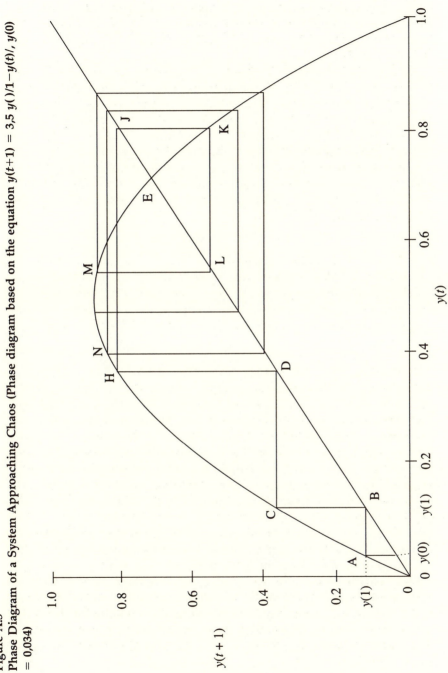

This diagram provides an example of a complex yet ordered time path. As the values of the main parameter are increased, the behavior of the system approaches chaos.

cycle makes its appearance. At further critical values of w, period-doubling occurs as each value in the period cycle generates two values. In this way, for some value of w, an infinite number of cycle lengths will be generated. The result is an oscillatory time path with no stable cycle (i.e., repeating) period.

An important matter, especially for forecasting purposes, is the sensitivity of such functions to initial conditions. That is, two time paths with similar initial points can give rise to radically divergent outcomes. For example, in the two cases cited above, for values $w = 3.935$ and $w = 3.94$, the time paths beginning from the identical values for $y(0)$ lead to totally unrecognizable phase diagrams after 30 periods.

The consequences for economics of chaos dynamics in complex systems have been to make forecasting extremely difficult. The two basic forecasting methods of extrapolation and of structural estimation have become inappropriate where:

- a time path might exhibit two-period oscillations of increasing amplitude for 30 periods, with the fluctuations all but disappearing for the next 30 periods, and then an explosive n-period cycle emerging abruptly thereafter;
- an error in calculation of the fifth decimal place of a parameter occurs—this can change the qualitative character of the forecast beyond all recognition.

Economists, and the business gurus that have built on quantitative approaches in economics, have responded by trying to increase the sophistication of their models. By adding more variables, more equations, and more data, and increasing processing speed, they have sought to understand the evolution of large and complex systems in all their detail and with maximum predictability. In one unintentionally amusing commentary on this search for detail, Baumol and Benhabib wrote that approaches to modeling chaos with applied time series "are complicated by the fact that the data sets used in reality are necessarily finite."[8] Indeed, this search for detail has been an impossible task at the extremes of a global system made up of corporations, economies, ecologies, and societies. Not even the largest supercomputer could cope with the myriad reactions and interactions it involves.

On a purely methodological level, chaos-modeling is intrinsically incapable of the deterministic, lawlike outcomes which conventional economics seeks, because it is inherently stochastic and blurs the distinction between randomness and determinism, and between order and disorder, and therefore contradicts the very heart and soul of the traditional economist's worldview.

NOTES

1. The reason for treating events in the real world as systems is that computing effects by looking at things as separate entities connected by causal relations becomes impossibly cumbersome when it comes to things with several variables and multiple connections among the variables. A human being is composed of some five octillion atoms, and his brain, of ten thousand million neurons. A hydrogen atom is composed of only one proton and one neutron in its nucleus and one electron in its shell, but the number of forces acting within it are so complex that multidimensional mathematics are needed to represent them. Cybernetician W. Ross Ashby showed that when one deals with really large numbers—for example, with ten billion nerve cells—or with intricate patterns of interaction—like those between species in the Amazon jungle—the combinatorial possibilities generate fantastically large numbers. Equally fantastic is the quantity of information processing demanded of a system that would compute the interactions. Physicist H. J. Bremermann argued that the upper bound of practical computability is the enormously large number 10^{70}, and this number is soon reached when one enters the combinatorial space of multiple variables in interaction. In the mathematics of computation, exponentials, factorials, and even more explosively increasing functions will soon appear. For this reason, it is quite impossible to explain the thoughts that pass through the mind of a person by summing the electrochemical discharges of the neurons in his brain, and even to compute the behavior of a corporation by summing the individual characteristics of its employees. Even in the case of a few variables with a limited degree of interaction numbers appear that are as great or greater than what can be realistically handled not only by our own "wetware," but even by sophisticated computational hardware and software. Consequently, scientists have learned to view individual interactions as part of the behavior of integrated wholes—complex *systems*. In this way, complexity in phenomena does not generate unmanageable complexity in understanding.

2. In a condition of equilibrium, the production of entropy, and forces and fluxes (the rates of irreversible processes) are all at zero, while in states near equilibrium entropy production is small, the forces are weak, and the fluxes are linear functions of the forces. Thus a state near equilibrium is one of *linear* nonequilibrium, described by linear thermodynamics in terms of statistically predictable behaviors, as the system tends toward the maximum dissipation of free energy and the highest level of entropy. Whatever the initial conditions, the system will ultimately reach a state characterized by the least free energy and the maximum of entropy compatible with its boundary conditions.

3. Change in the entropy of the systems is defined by the well-known Prigogine equation $dS = d_iS + d_eS$. Here dS is the total change of entropy in the system, while d_iS is the entropy change produced by irreversible processes within it, and d_eS is the entropy transported across the system boundaries. In an isolated system dS is always positive, for it is uniquely determined by d_iS, which necessarily grows as the system performs work. However, in an open system d_eS can offset the entropy produced within the system and may even exceed it. Thus dS in an open system need not be positive: it can be zero or negative. The open system

can be in a stationary state ($dS = 0$), or it can grow and complexify ($dS < 0$). Entropy change in such a system is given by the equation $d_eS = (-d_iS \leq 0)$; that is, the entropy produced by irreversible processes within the system is shifted into the environment.

4. Free energy in a system is inversely related to entropy, as given by the equation $F = E - TS$ (where F is free energy, E is total energy, T is absolute temperature, and S is entropy). At any given temperature, the smaller the system's entropy the greater its free energy, and vice versa.

5. The reader can create his or her own Bénard-cell experiment in the kitchen or pantry. The simplest way, we found, is to heat some cooking oil in a flat pan over a low heat. This creates a temperature gradient between the bottom and the top of the liquid. To see the Bénard cells, it is enough to add a granular powder, spreading it evenly over the surface. The grains of the powder will organize themselves into hexagonal cells, as heat flow in the liquid changes from simple conduction to more efficient convection.

6. Chemistry sheds further light on how systems of interacting elements move from states at or near equilibrium to the domains of nonequilibrium characteristic of open systems in the third state. Under controlled laboratory conditions, sets of chemical reactions are irradiated and forced to move progressively further from chemical equilibrium. Relatively near chemical equilibrium, the reaction system is still successfully described by solving the chemical kinetic equations that apply at equilibrium as well as those that correspond to the Brownian motion of the molecules and the random mixing of the components. But, as reaction rates are increased, at some point the system becomes unstable and new solutions are required to explain its state, branching off from those that apply near equilibrium. The modified solutions signify new states of organization in the system of reactants: stationary or dynamic patterns of structure, or chemical clocks of various frequency. Where the equilibrium branch of the solution becomes unstable, the reaction system acquires characteristics typical of nonequilibrium systems in general: coherent behavior appears, and a higher level of autonomy vis-à-vis the environment. The elements cohere into an identifiable unity with a characteristic spatial and temporal order; there is now a dynamic system, whereas near equilibrium there were but sets of reactants.

7. There are two varieties of catalytic cycles: cycles of autocatalysis, where a product of a reaction catalyzes its own synthesis; and cycles of cross-catalysis, where two different products (or groups of products) catalyze each other's synthesis. An example of autocatalysis is the reactions scheme $X + Y \rightarrow 2X$. Starting from one molecule of X and one of Y, two molecules of X are catalyzed. The chemical rate equation for this reaction is $dX/dt = k\,X\,Y$. When Y is held at a constant concentration, there is an exponential growth in X. Cross-catalytic reaction cycles have been studied in detail by the school of Ilya Prigogine. A model of such reactions, known as the Brusselator, consists of the following four steps:

(1) $A \rightarrow X$
(2) $B + X \rightarrow Y + D$
(3) $2X + Y \rightarrow 3X$
(4) $X \rightarrow E$

In this reaction model, X and Y are intermediate molecules within an overall sequence through which A and B become D and E. In step (2) Y is synthesized from X and B, while in step (3) an additional X is produced through collisions of $2X$ and Y. Thus while (3) in itself constitutes autocatalysis, (2) and (3) combine to make cross-catalysis.

8. William Baumol and Jess Benhabib, "Chaos: Significance, Mechanism, and Economic Applications," *Journal of Economic Perspectives* (Winter 1989): 77–106.

Selected Bibliography

STANDARD AND RECENT WORKS

Abraham, Ralph, and C. Shaw. *Dynamics: The Geometry of Behavior*. Santa Cruz, Calif.: Aeriel Press, 1984.

Ashby, W. Ross. *An Introduction to Cybernetics*. London: Chapman & Hall; New York: Barnes & Noble, 1956.

Beer, Stafford. *Platforms of Change*. New York: John Wiley, 1979.

Beishon, J., and G. Peters. *Systems Behavior*. New York: Open University Press, 1972.

Bertalanffy, Ludwig von. *General System Theory: Essays on Its Foundation and Development* (rev. ed.). New York: George Braziller, 1968.

Blauberg, I. V., V. N. Sadovsky, and E. G. Yudin. *Systems Theory: Philosophical and Methodological Problems*. Moscow: Progress Publishers, 1977.

Boulding, Kenneth E. *Ecodynamics, A New Theory of Societal Evolution*. Beverly Hills, Calif., and London: Sage, 1978.

Bowler, T. Downing. *General Systems Thinking: Its Scope and Applicability*. New York: Elsevier–North Holland, 1981.

Buckley, Walter, ed. *Modern Systems Research for the Behavioral Scientist*. Chicago: Aldine, 1968.

Cavallo, Roger E., ed. *Systems Research Movement: Characteristics, Accomplishments, and Current Developments*. Louisville, Ky.: Society for General Systems Research, 1979.

Chaisson, Eric J. *Cosmic Dawn: The Origin of Matter and Life*. Boston: Atlantic, Little, Brown, 1981.

Checkland, Peter. *Systems Thinking, Systems Practice*. New York: John Wiley, 1981.

Churchman, C. West. *The Systems Approach* (rev. and updated). New York: Harper & Row, 1979.

Club of Rome, Council of. *The First Global Revolution* (written by Bertrand Schnei-
    der and Alexander King). New York: Pantheon Books, 1991.
Corning, Peter A. *The Synergism Hypothesis, A Theory of Progressive Evolution.* New
    York: McGraw-Hill, 1983.
Csanyi, Vilmos. *General Theory of Evolution.* Durham, N.C., and London: Duke
    University Press, 1989.
Davidson, Mark. *Uncommon Sense: The Life and Thought of Ludwig von Bertalanffy.*
    Foreword by R. Buckminster Fuller, Introduction by Kenneth E. Boulding.
    Los Angeles: J. P. Tarcher, 1983.
Demerath, N. J., and R. A. Peterson, eds. *System, Change and Conflict.* New York:
    Free Press, 1967.
Eigen, Manfred, and P. Schuster. *The Hypercycle: A Principle of Natural Self-
    Organization.* New York: Springer, 1979.
Eldredge, Niles. *Time Frames.* New York: Simon and Schuster, 1985.
Eldredge, Niles, and Stephen J. Gould. "Punctuated Equilibria: An Alternative
    to Phylogenetic Gradualism." In R. Schopf, ed., *Models in Paleobiology.* San
    Francisco: Freeman, Cooper, 1972.
Falk, Richard, Samual S. Kim, and Saul H. Mendlovitz, eds. *Toward a Just World
    Order.* Boulder, Colo.: Westview Press, 1982.
Foerster, Heinz von, and George W. Zopf, Jr. *Principles of Self-Organization.* Ox-
    ford and New York: Pergamon Press, 1962.
Fuller, Buckminster. *Operating Manual for Spaceship Earth.* Carbondale, Ill.: South-
    ern Illinois University Press, 1970.
Gharajedaghi, Jamshid. *Toward a Systems Theory of Organization.* Seaside, Calif.:
    Intersystems Publications, 1985.
Glansdorff, P., and I. Prigogine. *Thermodynamic Theory of Structure, Stability and
    Fluctuations.* New York: Wiley Interscience, 1971.
Gray, William, and Nicolas Rizzo, eds. *Unity Through Diversity* (2 vols.). New
    York: Gordon & Breach, 1973.
Haken, Hermann. *Synergetics.* New York: Springer, 1978.
Haken, Hermann, ed. *Dynamics of Synergetic Systems.* New York: Springer, 1980.
Jantsch, Erich. *Design for Evolution.* New York: Braziller, 1975.
Jantsch, Erich. *The Self-Organizing Universe.* Oxford: Pergamon Press, 1980.
Jantsch, Erich, and Conrad H. Waddington, eds. *Evolution and Consciousness.*
    Reading, Mass.: Addison-Wesley, 1976.
Katchalsky, Aharon, and P. F. Curran. *Nonequilibrium Thermodynamics in Biophys-
    ics.* Cambridge, Mass.: MIT Press, 1965.
Katsenelinboigen, Aron. *Some New Trends in System Theory.* Seaside, Calif.: Inter-
    systems Publications, 1984.
Klir, George J., ed. *Trends in General Systems Theory.* New York: Wiley Intersci-
    ence, 1972.
Koestler, Arthur, and J. R. Smythies, eds. *Beyond Reductionism: New Perspectives
    in the Life Sciences.* London and New York: Macmillan, 1969.
Margenau, Henry, ed. *Integrative Principles of Modern Thought.* New York: Gordon
    & Breach, 1972.
Maturana, Humberto R., and Francisco Varela. *Autopoietic Systems.* Urbana, Ill.:
    Biological Computer Laboratory, University of Illinois, 1975.
Nappelbaum, E. L., Yu A. Yaroshevskii, and D. G. Zaydin. *Systems Research:*

Methodological Problems. USSR Academy of Sciences, Institute for Systems Studies. Oxford and New York: Pergamon Press, 1984.

Nicolis, G., and I. Prigogine. *Self-Organization in Non-Equilibrium Systems.* New York: Wiley Interscience, 1977.

Pattee, Howard, ed. *Hierarchy Theory: The Challenge of Complex Systems.* New York: Braziller, 1973.

Prigogine, Ilya, and I. Stengers. *Order Out of Chaos* (La Nouvelle Alliance). New York: Bantam, 1984.

Rapoport, Anatol. *General System Theory: Essential Concepts and Applications.* Cambridge, Mass.: Abacus Press, 1986.

Salk, Jonas. *The Anatomy of Reality.* New York: Columbia University Press, 1984.

Salk, Jonas. *The Survival of the Wisest.* New York: Harper & Row, 1973.

The Science and Praxis of Complexity. Tokyo: The United Nations University, 1985.

Simon, Herbert A. *The Sciences of the Artificial.* Cambridge, Mass.: MIT Press, 1969.

Thom, René. *Structural Stability and Morphogenesis.* Reading, Mass.: Benjamin, 1972.

Varela, Francisco J. "Autonomy and Autopoiesis." In Gerhard Roth and Helmut Schwegler, eds., *Self-Organizing Systems: An Interdisciplinary Approach.* Frankfurt: Campus Verlag, 1981.

Weiss, Paul A. et al. *Hierarchically Organized Systems in Theory and Practice.* New York: Hafner, 1971.

Whyte, L. L., A. G. Wilson, and D. Wilson, eds. *Hierarchical Structures.* New York: American Elsevier, 1969.

Wiener, Norbert. *The Human Use of Human Beings: Cybernetics and Society* (2nd ed.). Garden City, N.Y.: Doubleday Anchor Books, 1954.

Zeeman, Christopher. *Catastrophe Theory.* Reading, Mass.: Benjamin, 1977.

SELECTED BOOKS BY ERVIN LASZLO (in order of date of publication)

Essential Society: An Ontological Reconstruction. The Hague: Martinus Nijhoff, 1963.

Individualism, Collectivism and Political Power: A Relational Analysis of Ideological Conflict. The Hague: Martinus Nijhoff, 1963. [also in Japanese]

Human Values and Natural Science (ed. with J. Wilbur). New York and London: Gordon & Breach, 1970.

Evolution and Revolution: Patterns of Development in Nature, Society, Culture and Man (ed. with R. Gotesky). New York and London: Gordon & Breach, 1971.

Emergent Man (ed. with J. Stulman). New York and London: Gordon & Breach, 1972.

Introduction to Systems Philosophy: Toward a New Paradigm of Contemporary Thought. New York and London: Gordon & Breach; Toronto: Fitzhenry & Whiteside, 1972; reprinted: Gordon & Breach, 1984; 2nd ed.: New York: Harper Torchbooks, 1973.

The Systems View of the World: The Natural Philosophy of the New Developments in the Sciences. New York: George Braziller, 1972; Toronto: Doubleday Canada, 1972; Oxford: Basil Blackwell, 1975. [also in Persian, Japanese, French, Chinese, Korean, and Italian]

The Relevance of General System Theory (ed.). New York: George Braziller, 1972.

A Strategy for the Future: The Systems Approach to World Order. New York: George Braziller, 1974. [also in Japanese and Korean]

The World System: Models, Norms, Applications (ed.). New York: George Braziller, 1974.

Goals for Mankind: A Report to the Club of Rome on the New Horizons of Global Community. New York: E. P. Dutton, 1977; Toronto & Vancouver: Clarke, Irwin, 1977; London: Hutchinson, 1977; rev. ed.: New York: New American Library Signet Books, 1978. [also in Italian, Spanish, Finnish, Japanese, and Serbo-Croatian]

Goals in a Global Community, Vol. I: Studies on the Conceptual Foundations (ed. with J. Bierman). Oxford and New York: Pergamon Press, 1977. *Vol. II: The International Values and Goals Studies* (ed. with J. Bierman). Oxford and New York: Pergamon Press, 1977.

The Inner Limits of Mankind: Heretical Reflections on Contemporary Values, Culture and Politics. Oxford and New York: Pergamon Press, 1978; rev. ed.: London: Oneworld Publications, 1989. [also in German, French, Italian, Chinese, and Korean]

The Objectives of the New International Economic Order (with R. Baker, E. Eisenberg, and V. K. Raman). New York: UNITAR and Pergamon Press, 1978; reprinted: 1979. [also in Spanish]

The Obstacles to the New International Economic Order (with J. Lozoya, J. Estevez, A. Bhattacharya, and V. K. Raman). New York: UNITAR and Pergamon Press, 1979. [also in Spanish]

The Structure of the World Economy and Prospects for a New International Economic Order (ed. with J. Kurtzman). New York: UNITAR and Pergamon Press, 1980. [also in Spanish]

Disarmament: The Human Factor (ed. with D. F. Keys). Oxford and New York: Pergamon Press, 1981.

Systems Science and World Order: Selected Studies. Oxford and New York: Pergamon Press, 1984.

Evolution: The Grand Synthesis. Boston and London: Shambhala New Science Library, 1987. [also in Italian, German, Chinese, Spanish, and French]

The New Evolutionary Paradigm (ed.). New York: Gordon & Breach, 1991.

The Age of Bifurcation: The Key to Understanding the Changing World. New York and London: Gordon & Breach, 1992. [also in German, Spanish, Chinese, French, and Italian]

The Evolution of Cognitive Maps: New Paradigms for the 21st Century (ed. with I. Masulli). New York: Gordon & Breach, 1992.

A Multicultural Planet: Diversity and Dialogue in Our Common Future. Report of an Independent Expert Group to UNESCO (ed.). Oxford: Oneworld, 1992. [also in French, German, and Italian]

The Creative Cosmos: Towards a Unified Science of Matter, Life, and Mind. Edinburgh: Floris Books, 1993. [also in French, Italian, Chinese, Portuguese, and Spanish]

The Choice: Evolution or Extinction: The Thinking Person's Guide to Global Problems. Los Angeles: Jeremy Tarcher/Putnam, 1994. [also in German, Chinese, Korean, and Hungarian]

Vision 2020: Restructuring Chaos for Global Order. New York: Gordon & Breach, 1994.

The Interconnected Universe: Conceptual Foundations of Transdisciplinary Unified Theory. Singapore and London: World Scientific Ltd., 1995.

Changing Visions: Human Cognitive Maps: Past, Present, and Future (with Robert Artigiani, Allan Combs, and Vilmos Csanyi). Westport, Conn.: Praeger Publishers; London: Adamantine Press, 1996.

Evolution: The General Theory (rev. and enl. ed.). Cresskill, N.J.: Hampton Press, 1996.

The Systems View of the World: A Holistic Vision for Our Time (rev. and enl. ed.). Cresskill, N.J.: Hampton Press, 1996.

The Whispering Pond: A Personal Guide to the Emerging Vision of Science. Dorset, U.K. and Rockport, Mass.: Element Books, 1996. [also in Italian, German, Portuguese, Hungarian, and Chinese]

Index

About the Authors

ERVIN LASZLO, considered the foremost exponent of systems philosophy and general evolution theory, is President of the International Society for Systems Sciences, Founder-Director of the General Evolution Research Group, Editor of *World Futures*, Associate Editor of *Behavioral Science*, and President of the Club of Budapest. He is the author of 62 books and over 300 articles, and has taught at Northwestern, Indiana, Princeton, and Yale universities, and at the State University of New York. His distinctions include several academic degrees and international awards as well as honorary Ph.D.s.

CHRISTOPHER LASZLO, holder of two master's degrees from Columbia University and a doctorate from the University of Paris X, is head of Business Development for Central Europe at Lafarge S.A., a Fortune 500 transnational company. Previously, he was senior consultant with Braxton Associates, a management consulting firm.